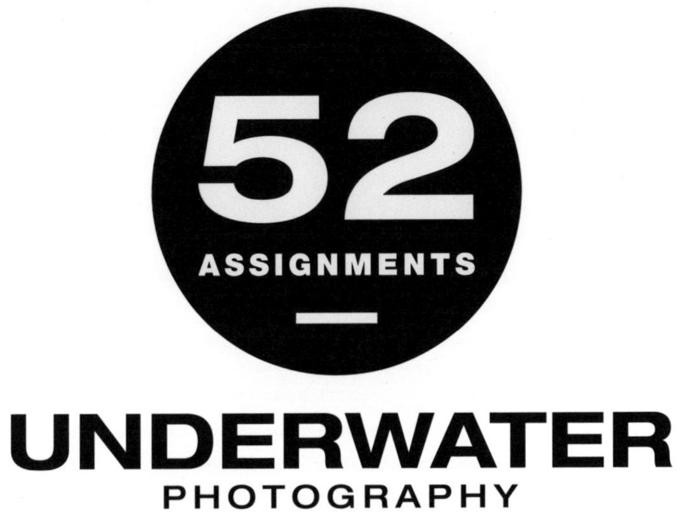

UNDERWATER
PHOTOGRAPHY

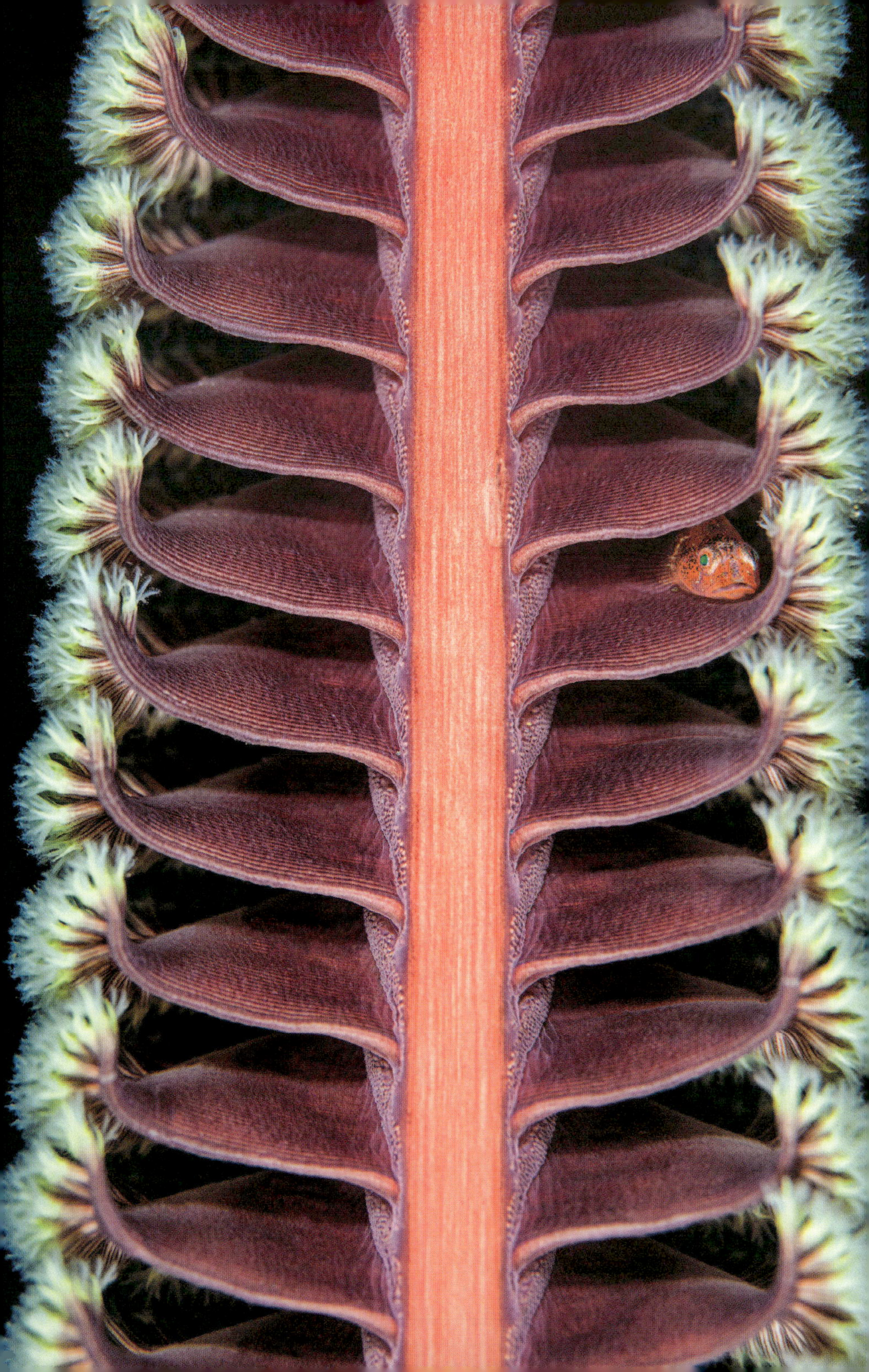

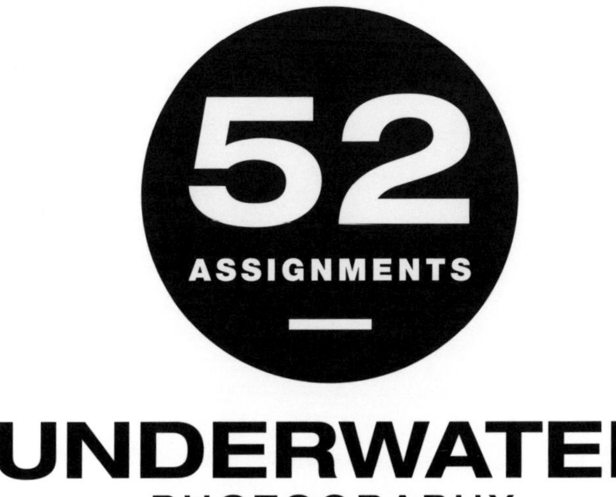

52 ASSIGNMENTS

UNDERWATER
PHOTOGRAPHY

ALEX MUSTARD

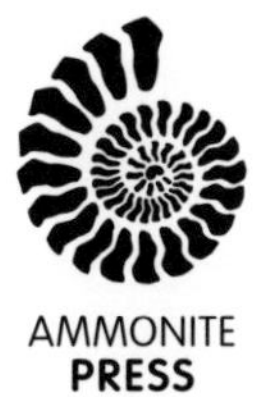

AMMONITE
PRESS

ASSIGNMENTS

Tick off your completed projects

- [ ] 01 AVAILABLE LIGHT FANTASTIC — 8
- [ ] 02 FLOAT LIKE A JELLY — 10
- [ ] 03 EARN THAT ANGLE — 12
- [ ] 04 SHOOT FROM THE HIP — 14
- [ ] 05 SUBJECT NOT SCENE — 16
- [ ] 06 ONE-STROBE MACRO — 18
- [ ] 07 COLOR COMBOS — 20
- [ ] 08 SILHOUETTES — 24
- [ ] 09 BLACK-AND-WHITE WRECKS — 26
- [ ] 10 VERTICALS ON THE SAND — 28
- [ ] 11 WIDEANGLE BLUES — 30
- [ ] 12 BOSSING DEPTH OF FIELD — 32
- [ ] 13 NATURAL PATTERNS — 34
- [ ] 14 BANG WITH BLACK — 36
- [ ] 15 WIDEANGLE MACRO — 38
- [ ] 16 VINTAGE LENSES — 40
- [ ] 17 CIRCULAR FISHEYE — 44
- [ ] 18 SPLITS WITHOUT A MASK — 46
- [ ] 19 SURFACE REFLECTIONS — 48
- [ ] 20 SNELL'S WINDOW — 50
- [ ] 21 MISSING THE BULLSEYE — 52
- [ ] 22 MANDARINFISH — 54
- [ ] 23 BLACKWATER — 56
- [ ] 24 SUMPTUOUS SUNBURSTS — 58
- [ ] 25 BEAM ME UP — 62
- [ ] 26 IN THE SPOTLIGHT — 64

ASSIGNMENT KEY

Each assignment has symbols showing the type of tasks involved.

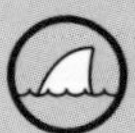 BIG ANIMAL

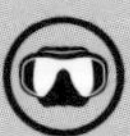 BUDDY

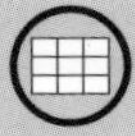 COMPOSITION

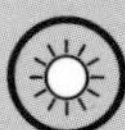 LIGHTING

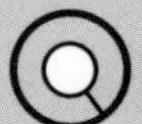 MACRO

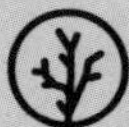 SCENERY

27	SNOOT WITH MOVEMENT	66
28	SIMPLE IS STRONG	68
29	GO SUPER	70
30	WORK WITH A GUIDE	72
31	SMALL IN THE FRAME	74
32	WORK THE BACKGROUND	76
33	OFF-CAMERA STROBE	78
34	FULL-COLOR WRECK	80
35	POSE A MODEL	82
36	LIGHT A MODEL	86
37	DOUBLE EYE CONTACT	88
38	MACRO BACKLIGHT	90
39	WIDEANGLE FLUORESCENCE	92
40	PAN-TASTIC	94
41	DIGITAL DOUBLES	96
42	ZOOM BLUR	100
43	HIGH-SPEED SYNCH	102
44	SUNSET SPLITS	104
45	PANORAMAS	106
46	PHOTOGRAMMETRY	110
47	MACRO FLASHLIGHT	112
48	DECISIVE MOMENT	114
49	WRONG LENS	116
50	COVER SHOT	118
51	TELL A STORY	120
52	RECIPE FOR SUCCESS	122

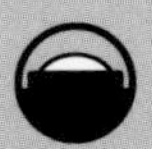 TECHNIQUE

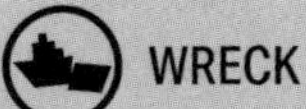 WIDEANGLE

WRECK

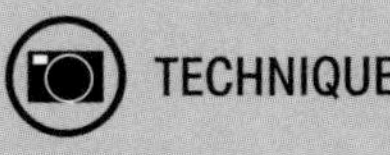 FISH

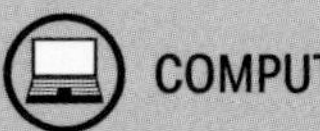 COMPUTER

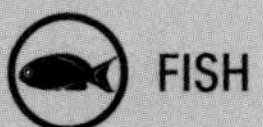

INTRODUCTION

This is a book to help you improve as an underwater photographer, but it isn't simply a book of methods. Instead, in these pages, you will find a series of assignments, challenges, ideas, exercises, gadgets, and even gear that I have especially suggested to expand your skills and horizons.

Many of you will be familiar with my popular book *Underwater Photography Masterclass*, which teaches you all the important techniques of underwater photography. This book is different, setting you specific assignments I have chosen to develop your skills. This isn't a book to simply read, it is a book for those who really want to develop skills and improve. It is intended that you read an assignment and then get in the water and work on it. Everyone can take snaps, but you need to apply yourself to make the most of your photographic potential. As David Doubilet puts it, "Just pushing a button is taking a photo. Thinking, lighting, and lots of other things—that's making a photo."

If you are new to shooting underwater then these 52 assignments will build a broad base of skills and experience across a diversity of genres. Alternatively, if you're already a seasoned shooter, this book is intended to invigorate. Many experienced photographers are frustrated that they are stuck shooting subjects in the same way; these challenges will kickstart your creativity, encouraging you to think differently and explore new types of underwater photography.

The books in this series present 52 assignments, which can be undertaken as weekly challenges. I'm aware that few photographers are fortunate to dive every week of the year, so I have crafted assignments that can mostly be completed in a dive or a suitable diving day. They are intended to be completed roughly in order, rather than you cherry-picking your favorites. If you do follow in sequence, you will find I've often alternated wideangle and macro topics to jolt you out of your comfort zone and keep you thinking.

Finally, underwater photographers often feel pressure to bring something back from every dive. When taking on these assignments, you will bring back something even more valuable: learning. It is the process, more than the results, that is the real reward from these assignments. To quote John Cleese, "Nothing will stop you from being creative so effectively as the fear of making a mistake." So, play, experiment, and have fun with these ideas and lessons—you are on the right course to exciting new underwater imagery.

Alex Mustard

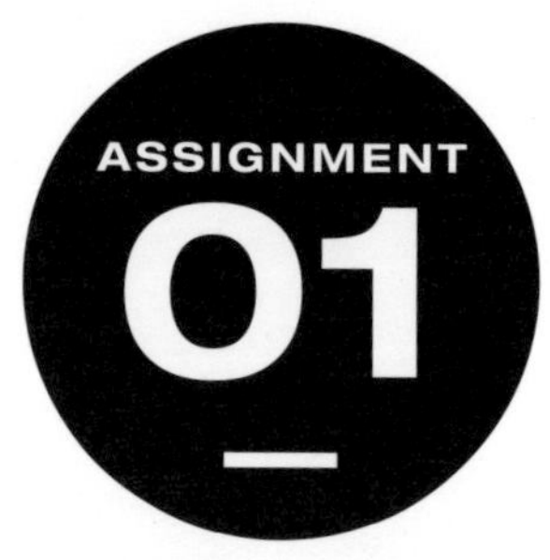

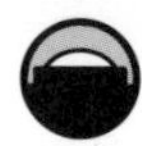
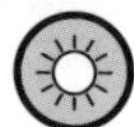
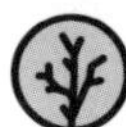

TIPS

- The direction of light has a massive impact on the look of your shots. Shoot with the light on your back for the best color in detail, and work across or against it for contrast and shadow.

- Without the instant burst of flash to freeze movement, keep your shutter speed at 1/90 sec. or faster.

- Auto-exposure modes do work with available light, but I suggest shooting in Manual mode, as light underwater is consistent and you will do less work dialing in Manual than constantly fiddling with the EV to get auto exposure to be correct on different scenes.

AVAILABLE LIGHT FANTASTIC

Your task for this assignment is to photograph in available light, and I don't mind what you shoot. Make use of what is served up by your diving or snorkeling. Available light suits shallow coralscapes, kelp and seaweed forests, big animals, pelagic action, wrecks, freedivers, and more. Your goal is to make strong compositions unencumbered by using flash.

When I suggest on my workshops that photographers dedicate their next dive to shooting in available light and leave their underwater flashguns on the boat, it always gets an unenthusiastic reaction. A hand inevitably goes up, followed by a "What if I see…?" question. Fear of missing out affects us all. Ironically, photographers concerned with missing a shot lose far more by skipping the challenge because few things will improve you more as an underwater photographer than a few dives shooting with only available light.

Underwater light is very different to on land. The height of the sun in the sky, clouds, sea state, visibility, and depth all impact on the photographic characteristics of light underwater. The more time you spend working with available light, the better placed you are to exploit it, even when also using flash in your images. So, while I hope you get some stunning available-light images, the reward of this assignment is more in the skills and knowledge you accumulate. Review your images, considering how they would have been different with flash.

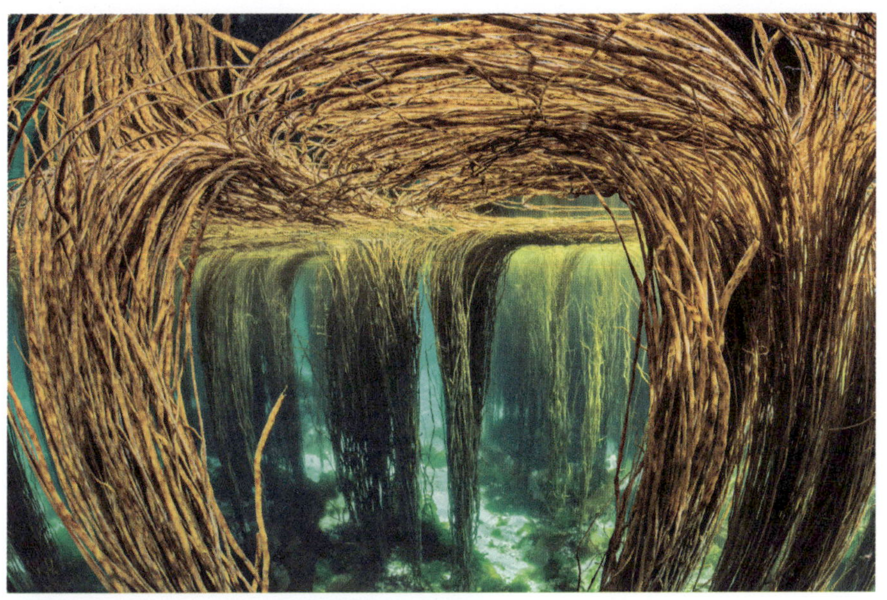

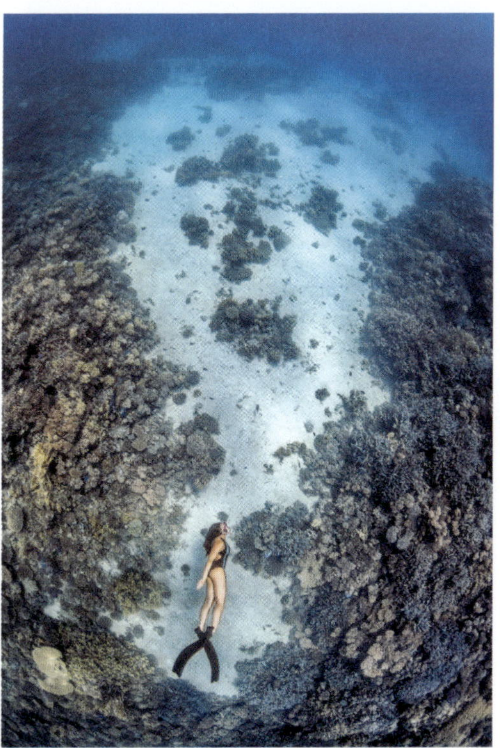

◄ ▲ Underwater photographers are so used to shooting with flashes, they often don't realize when it is better to switch them off.

PRO TIPS

- Underwater light comes down mainly from above, so pointing the camera upward or downward has a big impact on the look of your shots. Point down for color and detail, point up for shadow and contrast.

- Plants such as kelp and seaweeds look their best backlit by the sun, so shoot from their shadow side toward the light to get them to light up. This is much more effective than trying to light them with your flashes.

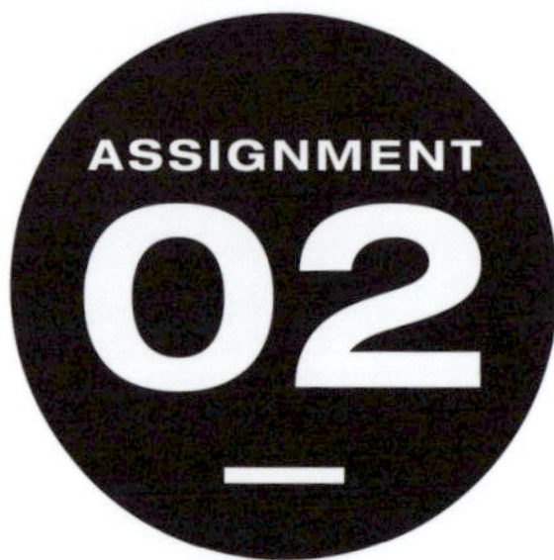

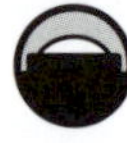

TIPS

- Jellyfish look great with the surface of the water in the picture, so try to include Snell's window (see Assignment 20) or reflections in the frame.

- Compose jellyfish with the sun directly behind them and they will glow like a light bulb.

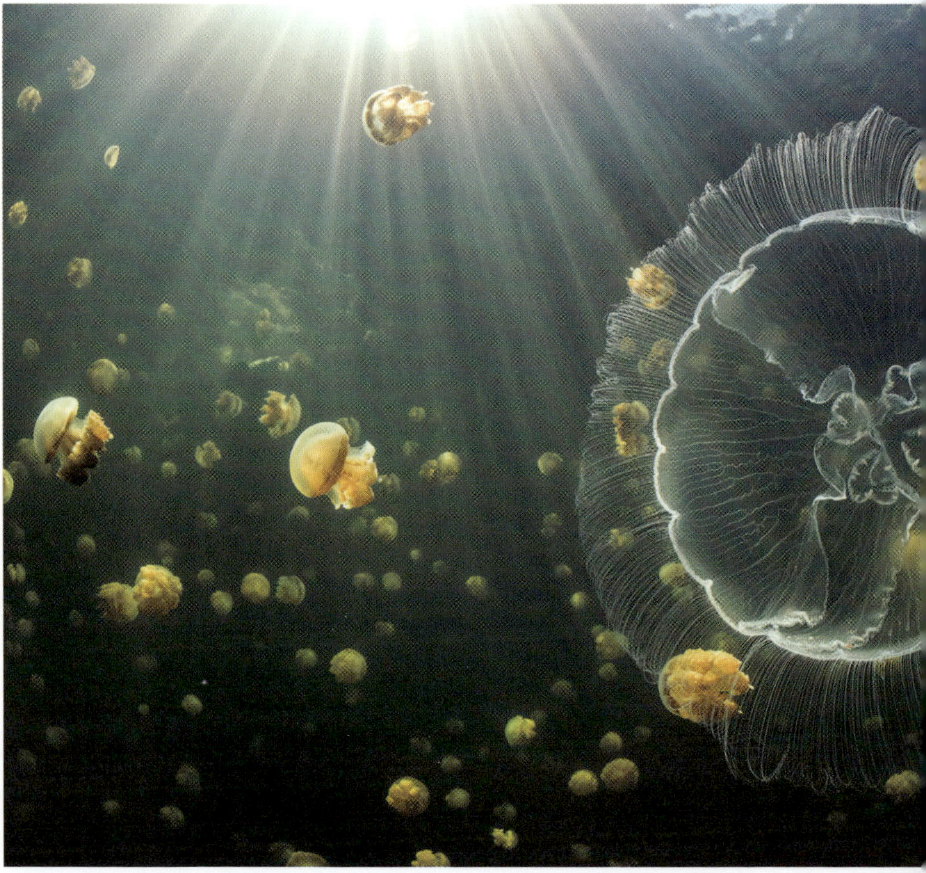

FLOAT LIKE A JELLY

I've long called jellyfish "judge's kryptonite" because of how regularly they are awarded in photographic contests. They are otherworldly and beautifully reflect light and transmit it through their translucent bodies. For this assignment, I want you to spend several dives shooting them.

Jellyfish look beautiful from a distance, but it can be hard to maneuver close enough to shoot them without disrupting their delicate form. If you approach unsteadily or quickly, you will create a bow wave that will distort their elegant shape or cause them to retract their tentacles. Good diving skills are a must with a mid-water subject, but equally important is having a well-balanced camera. Underwater photography gear is bulky and heavy, but it doesn't have to be when you are underwater.

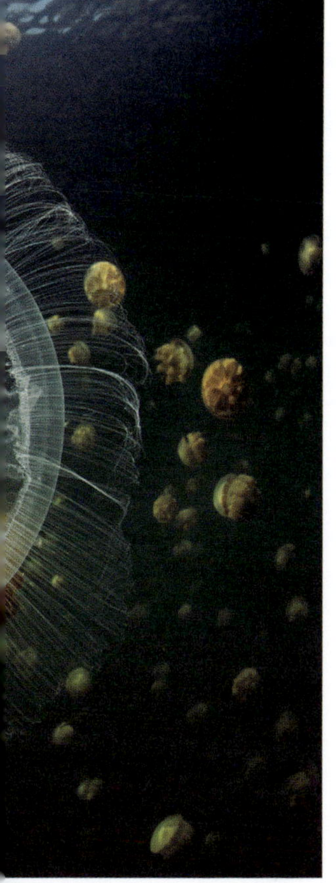

After you have shot some jellies, spend some time optimizing the buoyancy and trim of your camera and go again. Compare both the ease of shooting and the results and hopefully you will be quickly convinced of the advantages of a neutrally buoyant camera for all your wideangle photography.

Cameras and housings are heavy and usually negatively buoyant. Fortunately, dome ports, especially larger ones, contain lots of air and most rigs are close to neutral with a large dome. You can add further buoyancy with floating strobe arms and buoyancy collars for ports. Large acrylic domes are very floaty, so attach a few adhesive wheel-balancing weights on the bottom shade of the port to trim the rig. On boat dives, a neutral rig is also a comfort because if accidentally dropped it won't sink to the depths. On shore dives, a neutral camera will just sit happily next to you while you put on your mask and fins.

◀ A neutral rig is stable. It lets you move more carefully around subjects and when near the seabed you won't stir up sediment. You will also be more comfortable while you wait for the perfect shot.

ASSIGNMENT 03

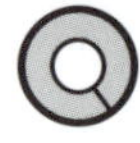
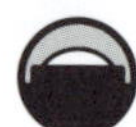
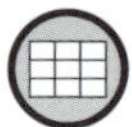

TIPS

- A 45º viewfinder is a valuable accessory because it allows us to shoot at eye level or even slightly upward while still holding a comfortable body position.

- Download your shots soon after diving and evaluate how those low-angle shots work best while your back is still aching. The goal of this assignment is to appreciate how much of the quality of a picture comes from making the very best of the opportunity by using the strongest angle.

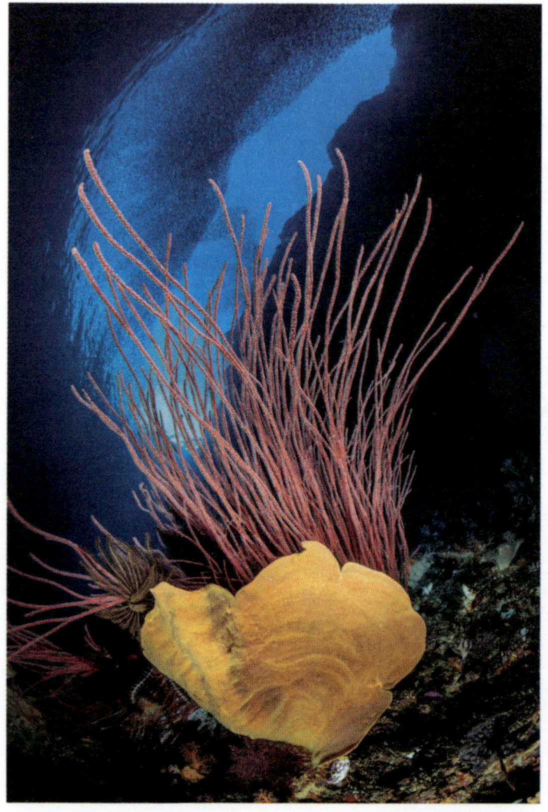

◀ *Shooting from below the subject allows you to include far more of the subject's wider environment.*

▶ *Many small animals live secret lives, so work to get the camera down to their level.*

EARN THAT ANGLE

Few factors improve an underwater photo like getting the camera close and down to the level of the subject. It's a win-win, giving you a better connection with the subject and at the same time better separation from the background. New photographers tend to shoot slightly down, as this is the natural angle that you spot the subject from as you swim over the seabed. But this tends to give poor eye contact and the subject also blends with the surroundings. The aim of this exercise is to break that habit, so your first reaction isn't to start shooting, but to stop and assess the options, reapproaching from the angle that will give the best picture.

For this assignment, don't expect the best photographic angle to be the easiest. Instead, put in the effort to contort your body, arch that back, and perhaps even hang upside down to unlock the best composition. If you are uncomfortable stretching and pushing for the best viewpoint, you can be reassured that other photographers will have already given up and you are on your way to standout images.

If you are shooting with a wideangle lens, getting down and even slightly below the main subject will make it jump out of the picture as well as introduce layers of attractive silhouetted scenery and water surface textures into the picture. For macro, the low angle will yield excellent eye contact with the subject and a clean background of either open water or distant, out-of-focus seabed.

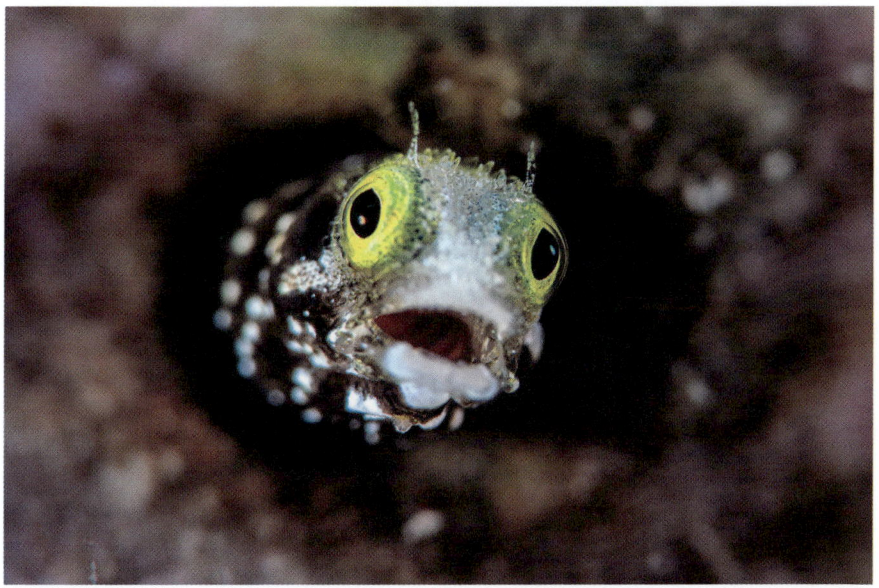

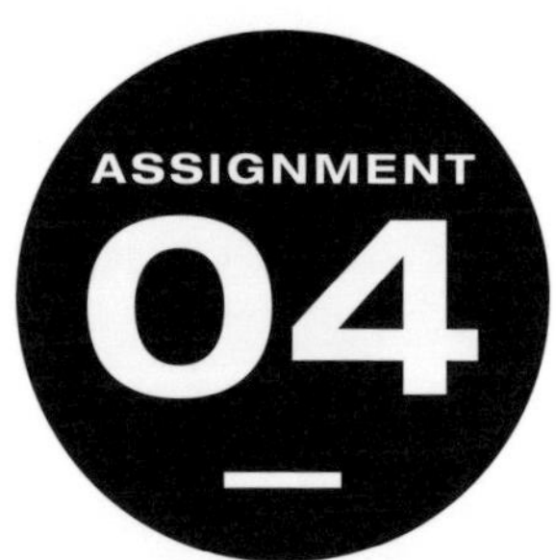

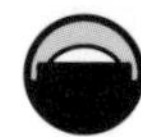
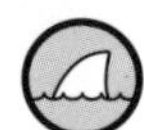
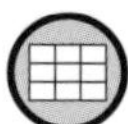
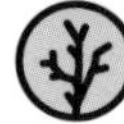

TIPS

- This technique works best with the widest lenses. Practicing with just one focal length is the best way to refine your skills. You can trust your normal wideangle autofocus settings to work, even when you are not looking through the camera.

- I always use a strap on the right handle of my housing, which holds my hand tight in place and allows me to shoot one-handed. It is also valuable for maintaining a consistent angle between my hand and where the lens is pointing, greatly increasing the accuracy of my shots from the hip.

SHOOT FROM THE HIP

Sometimes, the best viewpoint for a wideangle shot is one where you can't get your eye to the viewfinder or even catch a glimpse of the LCD screen. But don't let this stop you—it's time to shoot blind. It sounds strange to set an assignment that encourages you not to look at what you are shooting, but if holding the camera away from you produces a better picture, it's worth it.

The first time you try this technique, you are likely to miss the composition you want, but the more you practice, the better your aim. Work at this technique to the point of being able to compose different elements very precisely with your favored lens. This is an assignment to revisit regularly whenever you have a few spare minutes on a wideangle dive. For example, when you are safety stopping, try shooting a frame with one diver close and one far away, both balanced in the picture. Shoot, review, and improve your aim.

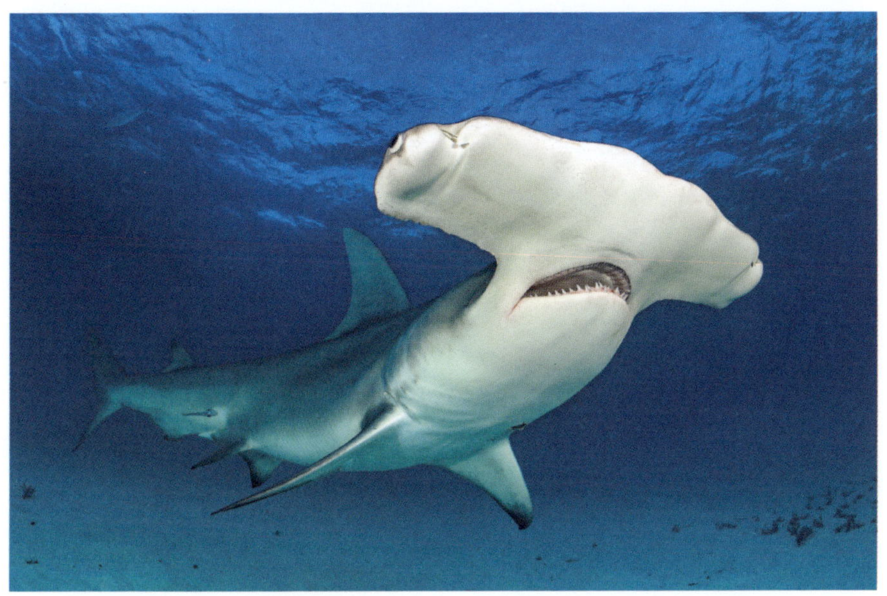

▲ *Shooting blind unlocks great angles and gets the camera closer to the action.*

There are many common underwater situations where shooting from the hip is advantageous, such as when a subject suddenly appears, and you have moments to grab a shot. Other examples are holding the camera beneath an overhang when shooting reef or holding the camera out to get it closer to a school of fish without disrupting their formation.

When shooting sharks, I regularly shoot from the hip because it is important to always be aware of what is going on around you. It is not a good idea to get stuck in your camera's viewfinder. Sharks typically stay close to the seabed and holding the camera down to their level separates them from the background. A common mistake is to aim the camera at the head of the shark, which will cut off the tail in the picture. Instead, aim the camera at the pectoral fins and the shark's body will be evenly balanced across the frame.

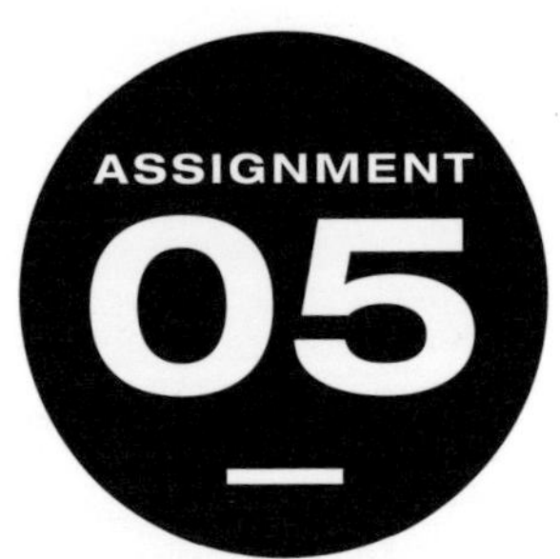

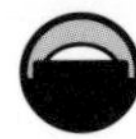

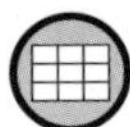
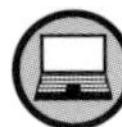

TIPS

- Despite being wideangle, you will need your strobes pulled in tight against your housing when shooting frame-fillers, often angled in toward the subject when you get very close.

- A small dome port aids lighting when close to the subject. With a big dome, there is always a minimum distance that you can evenly light the subject.

- Stop the lens down more than usual to keep background details sharp.

▶ *Feed your fisheye with a frame-filling subject and let the scene unfold around it.*

SUBJECT NOT SCENE

Wideangle lenses, especially fisheyes, are the most powerful optics for eye-catching underwater imagery because they allow you to shoot big scenes through as little water as possible. However, their wide field of view will readily make your scenic photos look like boring backgrounds waiting for a subject, unless you provide a main subject for the composition. For this challenge, you need to use your widest lens, and with it spend the dive shooting frame-filling compositions. Compositionally, is it possible to get too close to your subject?

It is natural to be drawn to attractive sections of the reef for pictures, but once there don't just shoot the scene. You always need to find a main subject to feed your fisheye and let the scene play out around it.

New underwater photographers mistakenly think that the barrel distortion of fisheye lenses is an undesirable feature, as it mostly is on land. Once underwater, fisheyes thrive because there are few straight lines, but more importantly, their distortion acts to magnify our strobe-lit foregrounds and push our backgrounds further away, creating a more three-dimensional and appealing perspective. You maximize this effect with a strong foreground subject.

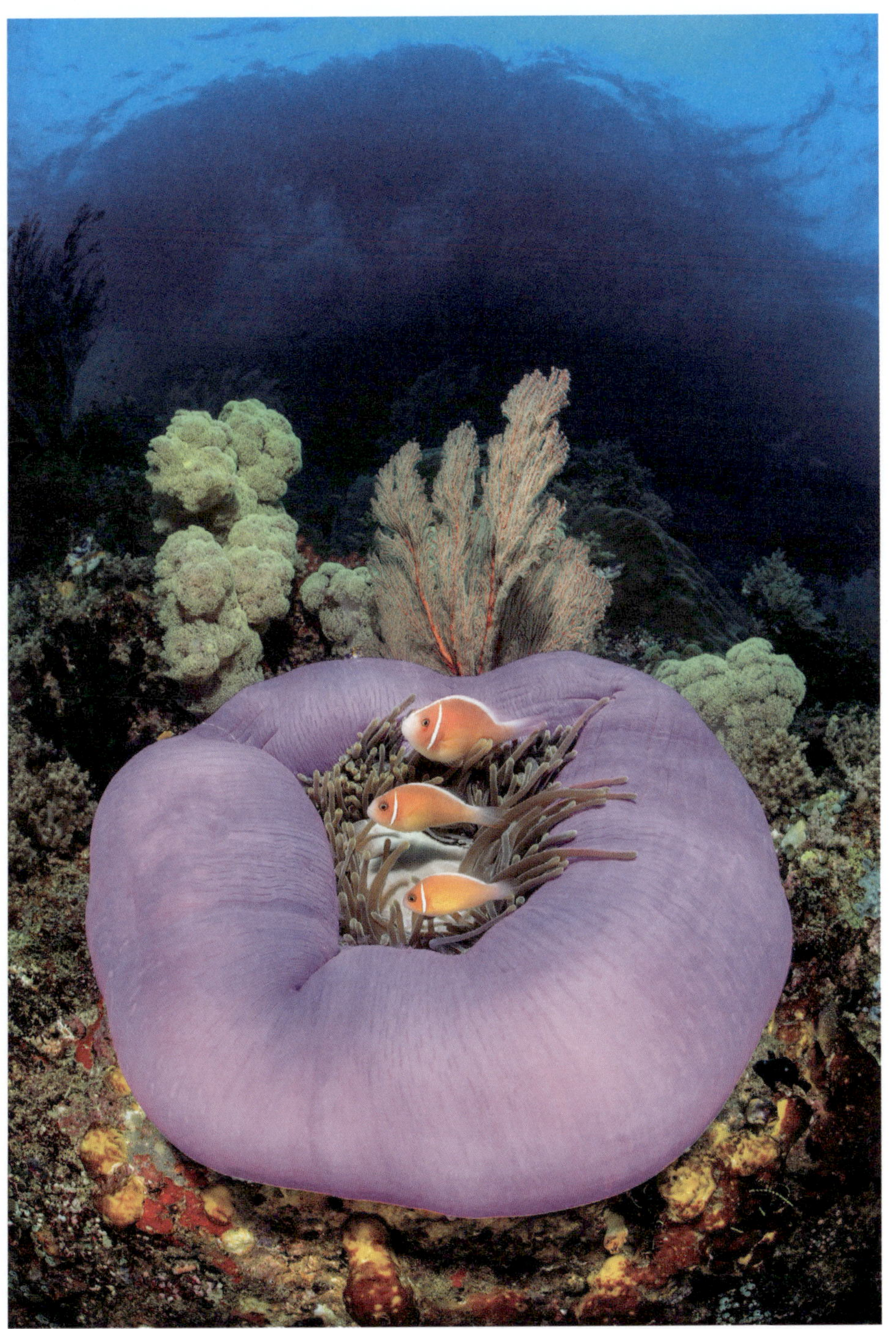

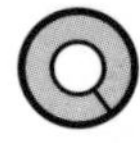
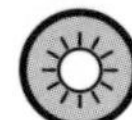

- Key to exploiting a single lighting source is moving it. De-clutter your housing, removing focus lights (unless essential) and action cameras, so you can move the strobe freely around each subject.

- Adding a beam restrictor—a short 0.75in (2cm) ring—onto the front of your flash will give you a harder, more directional light, better for revealing shape and texture when side lighting.

ONE-STROBE MACRO

Once underwater photographers buy a second flash, they rarely shoot single-strobe again. There are many reasons why working with a pair of strobes is highly desirable, but this exercise is to remind you that one strobe can rule, especially in macro. The key to this assignment is to fit only one strobe onto your camera and use two sections of strobe arms, so that you can move it around freely. Some shots will be easy, others will be a challenge, but the learning comes when you must think and experiment to get the lighting you want.

Single-strobe shooting is especially suited to subjects that live on sediment. In reef environments, I usually prefer to shoot macro with two strobes to create evenly lit portraits. However, on muck dives, I prefer the ability to be more selective with my lighting, illuminating what is interesting and hiding what isn't. The directional light from a single strobe is also ideal for accentuating the monstrous characteristics of the species you'll find here.

The goal of this assignment is to see how different strobe positions impact on the look of a subject and its surroundings, which is easier to appreciate with a single strobe. I hope this assignment brings some strong images and encourages you to regularly switch off one of your flashes on future macro dives.

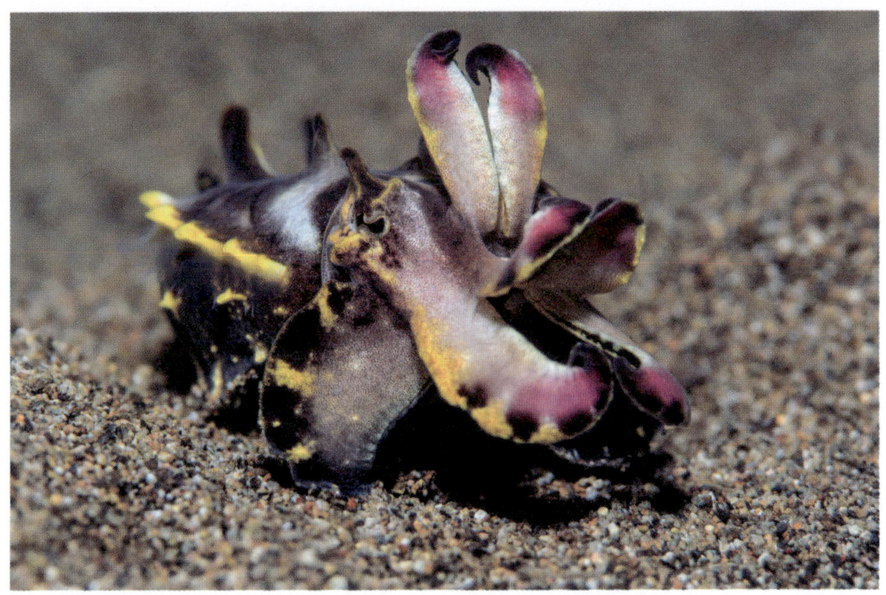

▲ To create even illumination with a single flash, with a small drop shadow below the subject, position your strobe above the port and point it forward.

▼ A more interesting use of single flash is to selectively light subjects. Angle the strobe in from an acute angle for shadowy side light, or push it beyond the subject for backlighting.

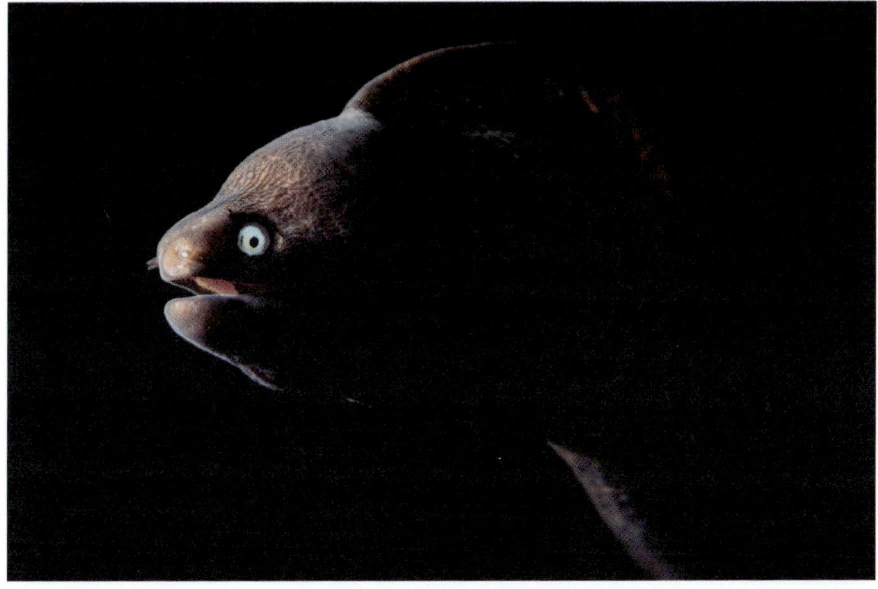

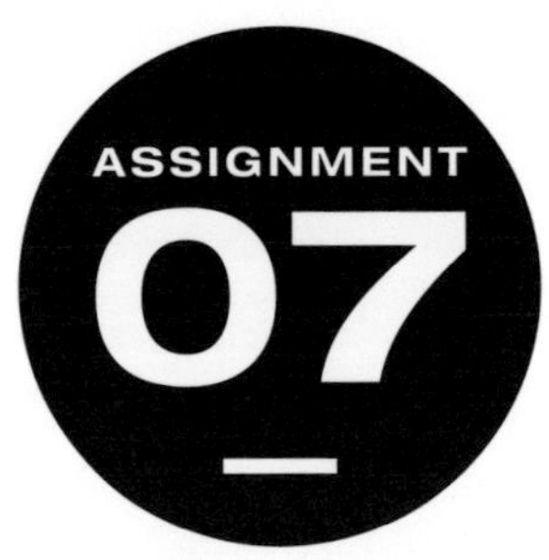

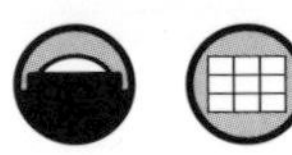

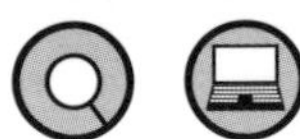

TIPS

- Lightroom gives you precise control over colors in the Color Mixer, which we can use to create harmonious or complementary relationships in your pictures.

- Colors are linked with emotion. Red is hot, exciting, dangerous, and impactful. Blue is peaceful, balanced, and calming.

- The underwater world is primarily blue, so whenever you find a warm-colored (red, orange, yellow) subject, always try to pair it with a blue-water background.

COLOR COMBOS

It is natural to be drawn to colorful subjects, especially so underwater where marine life from the tropics to the poles can be painted in the richest of hues. The aim of this assignment is to improve your use of color. I am challenging you to make a dive where the focus isn't finding animals, but finding and photographing different color combinations. I want you to seek out examples of both harmonious colors and complementary colors underwater.

A standard color wheel displays colors graphically, illustrating how primary colors combine to create secondary colors and other hues. It is useful for photographers because it reveals the relationships between various colors and helps you exploit these in both your shooting and processing. Harmonious colors are combinations from adjacent areas of the color wheel and work pleasingly together and are satisfying to the eye. Examples of harmonious shots are green kelp growing in blue water, or pink goby living in a red soft coral.

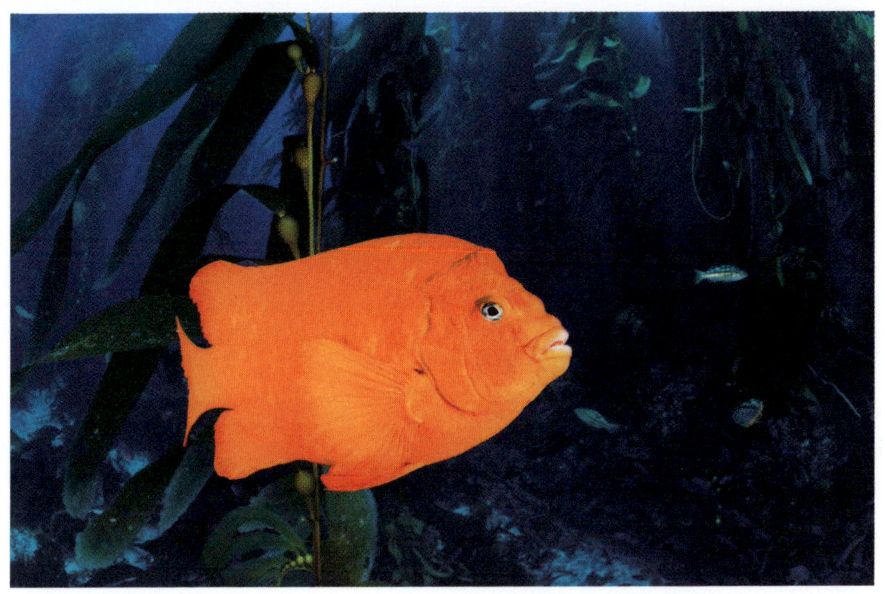

▲ *An orange garibaldi swimming through the blues and greens of a kelp forest jumps out thanks to classic complementary colors.*

Complementary colors are from opposite sides of the color wheel and strongly contrast, creating images with impact. A classic example is red soft coral and orange anthias framed against the Red Sea's blue water, or the yellow stripes set against the blue body of an emperor angelfish. Both approaches yield strong images and making color the focus of a few dives will benefit your photographic approach long term.

Color theory is even more valuable when processing images because you have more time to consider the relationships between colors on the picture and detailed processing tools to selectively adjust individual hues. For instance, if you want a main subject to stand out from the background of cool blue water, you can push the foreground hues to warmer colors and even cool down the water behind, thus exaggerating the difference. In another shot, you could choose a more harmonious color palette by processing the image so foreground and background colors converge on the same side of the color wheel.

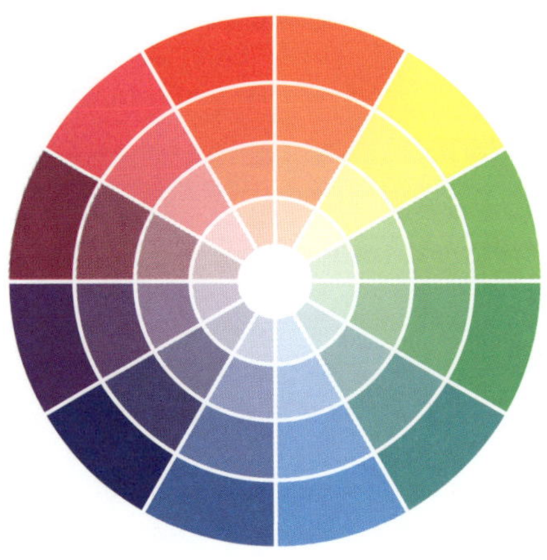

▼ *Greens and blues are common underwater and if you limit the color palette to these harmonious combinations, it produces peaceful pictures. You wouldn't want an entire portfolio filled with these more subtle images, but they provide a valued change of pace in an exhibition or presentation.*

▶ *Temperate waters are usually more green than blue. In such conditions, the complementary color for foregrounds moves away from yellows, oranges, and reds and toward pinks and purples. This pink lion's mane jellyfish contrasts well against the greens in this frame.*

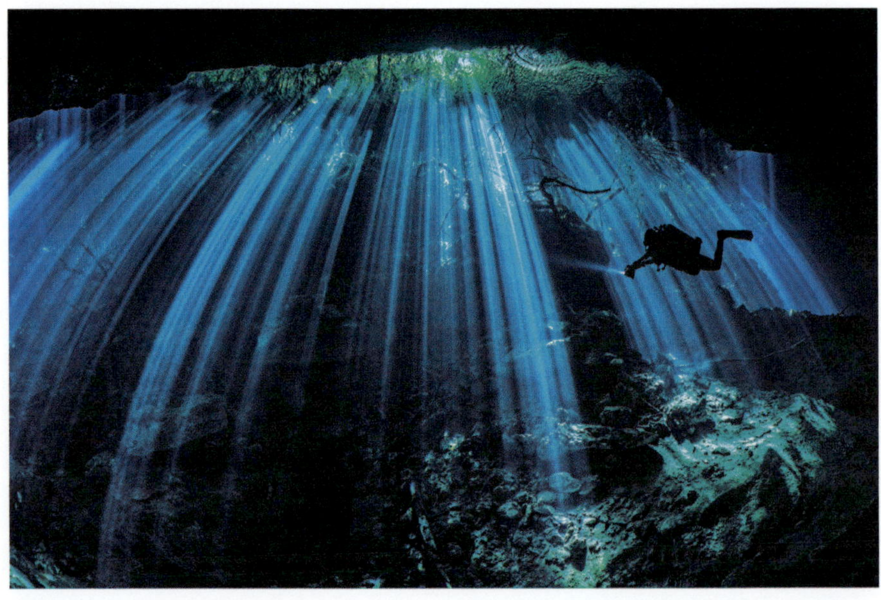

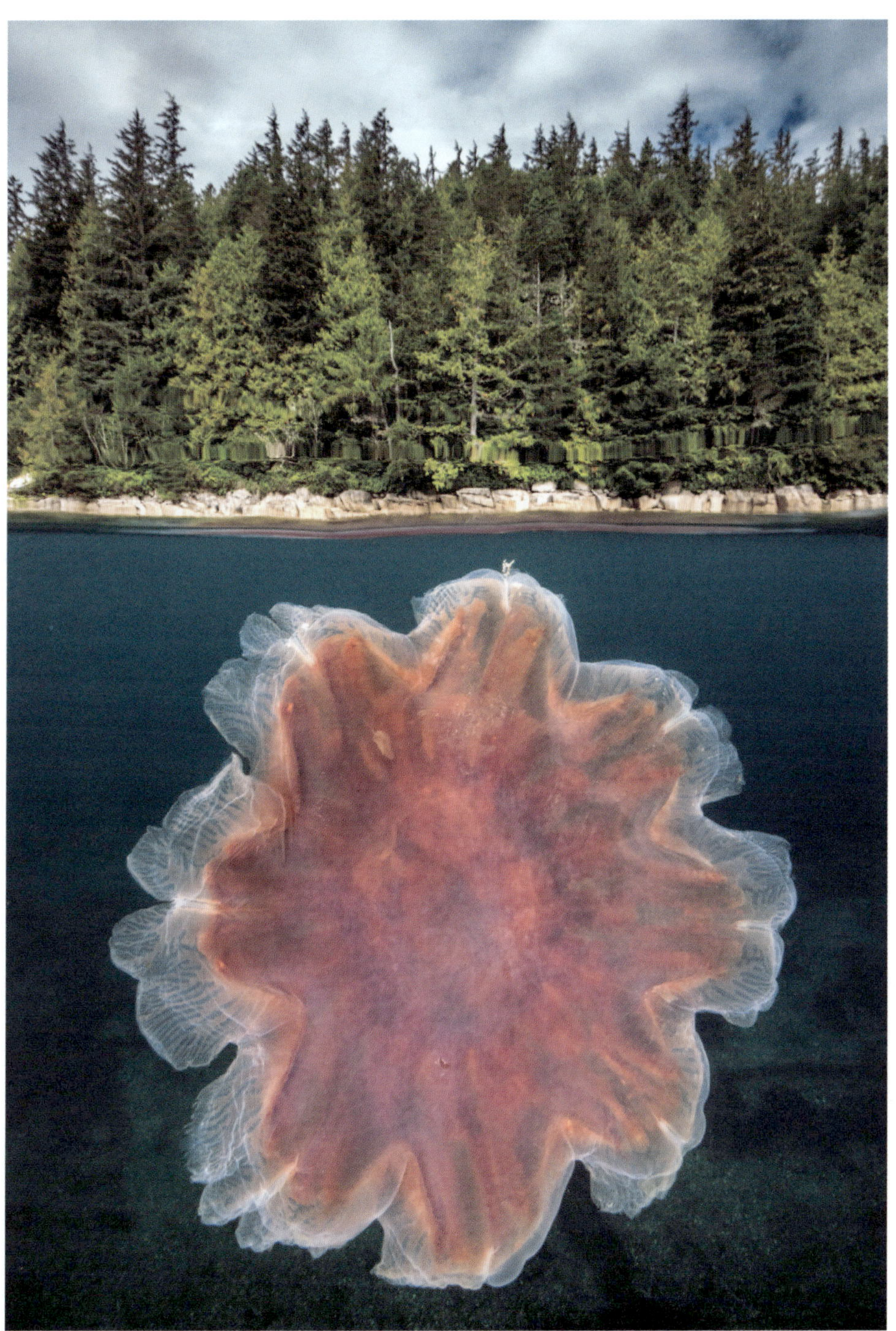

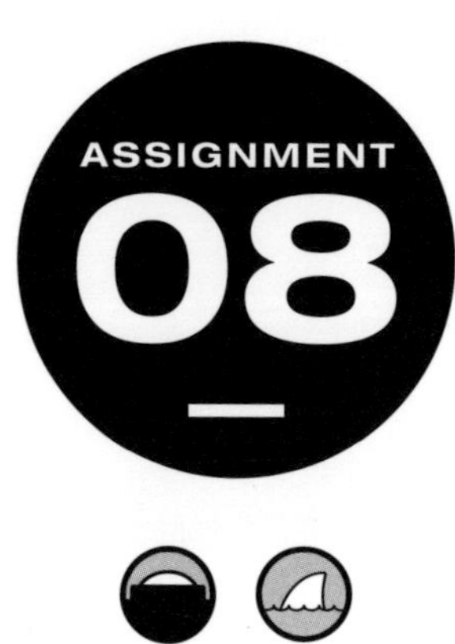

TIPS

- Silhouettes are typically wideangle shots underwater but try the technique with macro as a creative alternative.

- It is common to shoot wideangle pictures against the light, as you usually fill the scene with flash to bring out the detail in the subject. For silhouettes, you simply turn off your flashes. It is often possible to shoot both on the same pass.

- On many cameras, you can set a custom button on your underwater housing to be a one-touch flash off. Alternatively, you can set up a custom shooting mode to be flash only, which can be activated with a twist of the mode dial.

SILHOUETTES

Bold and impactful, silhouettes are valuable additions to any portfolio. Nature photographers on land regard these among the hardest shots to get because they need to find a subject framed against the sun at the start or end of the day. Underwater, both the subject and photographer can move freely in three dimensions, so you can simply drop below a creature to frame it against the sun. Also, since most underwater pictures are made with flash, silhouettes are an easy technique. You don't even have backscatter to worry about. In fact, underwater silhouettes are so straightforward that many underwater photographers feel they are beneath them, which is a big mistake. The aim of this assignment is to put silhouettes firmly on your wish list of shots from any destination.

Choosing subjects that are easily recognizable and graphically interesting as an outline is key to this technique. Classic underwater examples include mantas, turtles, schools of fish, table corals, and other divers, but other subjects such as wrecks, sharks, dolphins, sea lions, and even individual fish can also work very well. If the subject is reasonably large and close, you can hide the sun behind it, creating strong contrast and a spray of sun beams shooting out on all sides. You can rehearse this shot by holding your hand in front of the lens to block the sun and dial in the camera settings for the correct exposure.

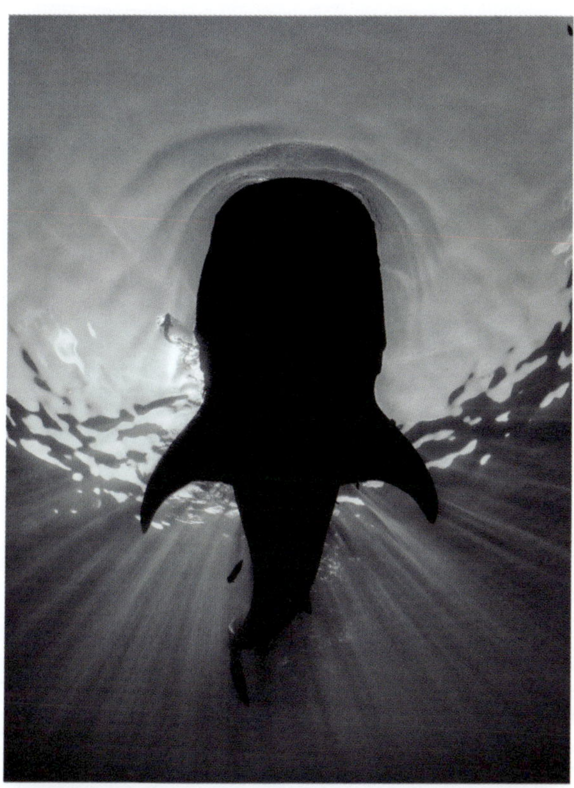

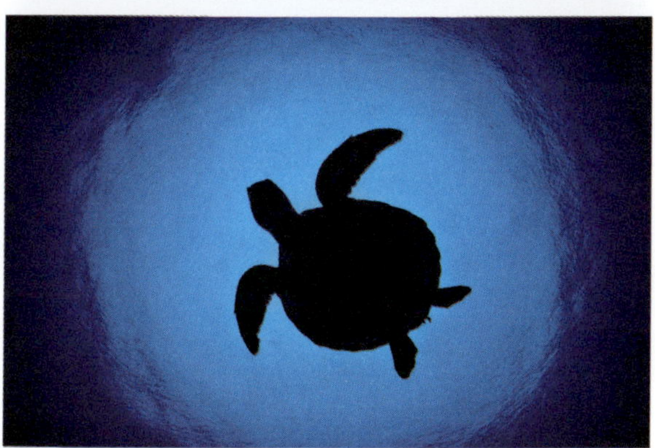

Snell's window, the circle formed when shooting up toward the surface, is often a vital element in silhouette shots, especially so in cloudy weather or when the sun is very low in the sky. In these conditions, the edge of Snell's window is most clearly defined and creates an attractive frame within the composition.

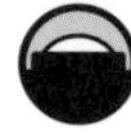

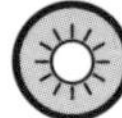
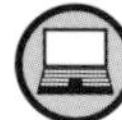

TIPS

- Drop low and shoot up to separate the wreck from the seabed.

- Shoot against or across the light to accentuate shadows, which will create strong black areas and reveal shape.

- Choose the monochrome mode and add some extra contrast. On a mirrorless camera, this will mean that both your viewfinder and your review images will be in black and white. On a DSLR, only your photos will be black and white. In both cases, this helps you to exploit the light to create stronger images. Your Raw files will still contain the color data.

▼ *A low camera angle separates the wreck and the bright water, boosting the contrast of the shot.*

▶ *Seek out shadows in your compositions by shooting across the light to add visual drama to the frame.*

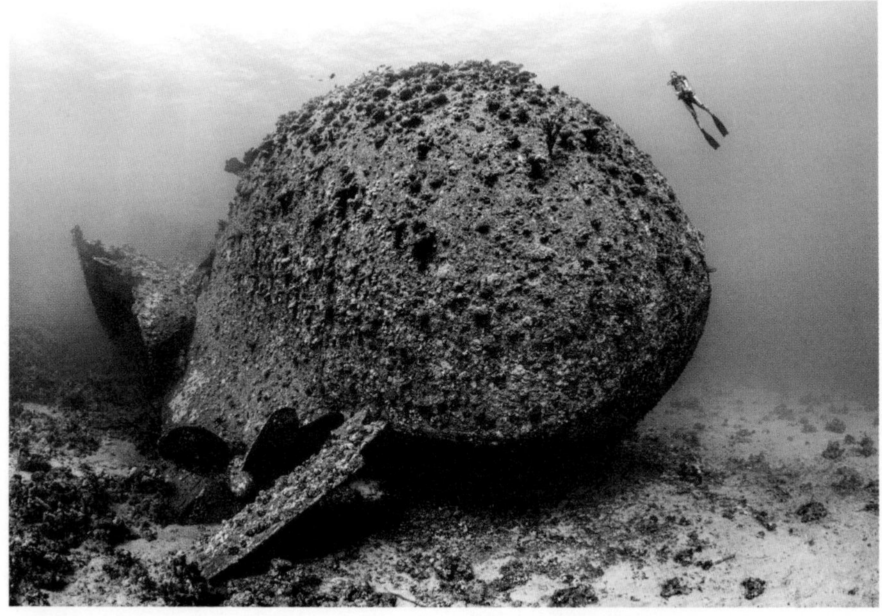

BLACK-AND-WHITE WRECKS

There is no doubt that shipwrecks look great in black and white. Monochrome suits
the historic and reflective atmosphere, while black-and-white processing allows
you to cut through the water and make the subject really pop. When color is taken
out of a photograph, the viewer is invited to explore the shapes and textures in the
composition, so your assignment is to home in on these elements.

Flash will be ineffective, so switch it off and make the most of the ambient light.
Shooting across and against the sun will mix areas of shadow with areas of detail,
which will look particularly good in a black-and-white conversion. Sinking close to
the seabed and shooting up guarantees that you are using the light in this way and
creates a bright water background, so the wreck stands out.

Processing black-and-white photos is quite different from processing other
underwater photos. There is plenty of room for creativity and, unusually, you can
be heavy-handed with the adjustment sliders. Your aim should be to avoid a sea of
gray and produce a picture with blacks and whites. The basic workflow is to fix white
balance first, so the wreck is a different color to the water, and then convert to black
and white and add lots of contrast and clarity. Finally, you can use the B & W sliders in
Lightroom to alter the tone of the different colors in the original file, allowing you to
brighten or darken the water relative to the wreck.

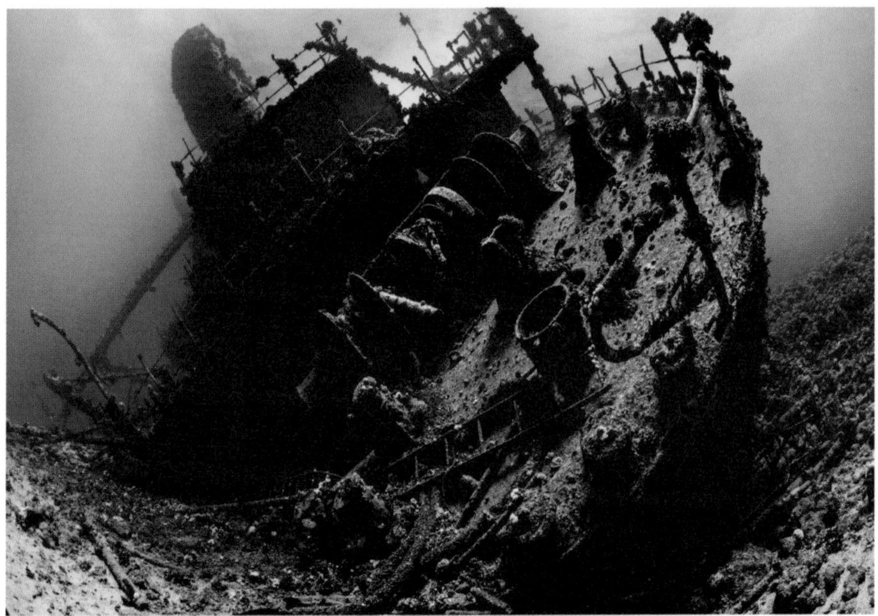

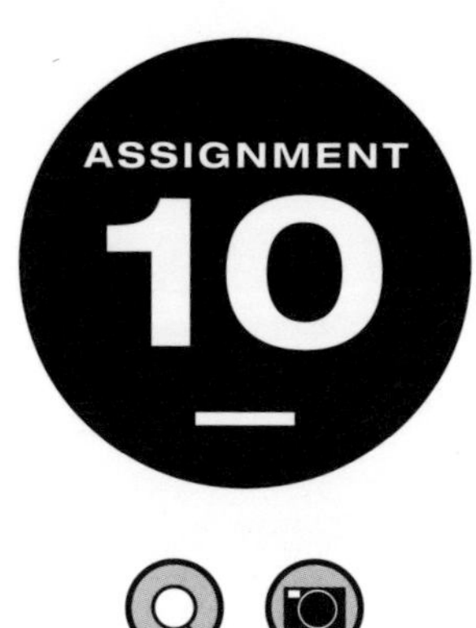

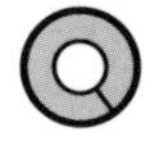

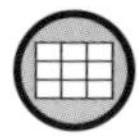

TIPS

- Underwater, your rig will be very easy to shoot, but it might be unstable on the boat. Make sure you have a secure place to park it between dives.

- You can still shoot horizontal images, but aim for verticals and make the most of your low-angle advantage.

- A 45° viewfinder is a big advantage when shooting low to the seabed, meaning you don't need to be as low as your camera.

▶ *The low angle improves eye contact with the subject and greatly enhances the separation from the background.*

VERTICALS ON THE SAND

As an underwater photographer, you quickly learn that when shooting macro subjects on the seabed, the lower you get the camera, the better the photo. This is easy to do when shooting horizontal images, but much more difficult for verticals because the bulk of the camera rig gets in the way. So, for this assignment, I want you to shoot seabed verticals, and to modify your housing setup specifically for the job. Any creature living on the seabed, such as nudibranchs, blennies, frogfish, and seahorses, will benefit from this approach. When I am on a muck-diving trip, I do this for the day, about every third or fourth day, so my trip portfolio has a mixture of standout horizontal and vertical shots.

All housings have the shutter release on the right side, and when shooting verticals on the sand, you want this to be at the top, so your hand isn't stopping the camera being as low as possible. Next, unbolt the handle on the left side of the housing and remove it. It doesn't matter if this is where you attach one of your strobe arms because the next step is to screw in a new strobe-mounting ball to the original base of the housing. Almost all housings have some sort of tripod-mounting thread on their base, and you can now mount the left-hand strobe and arm here. The result is a setup that defaults to shooting verticals and can be used from a significantly superior viewpoint than other photographers can achieve.

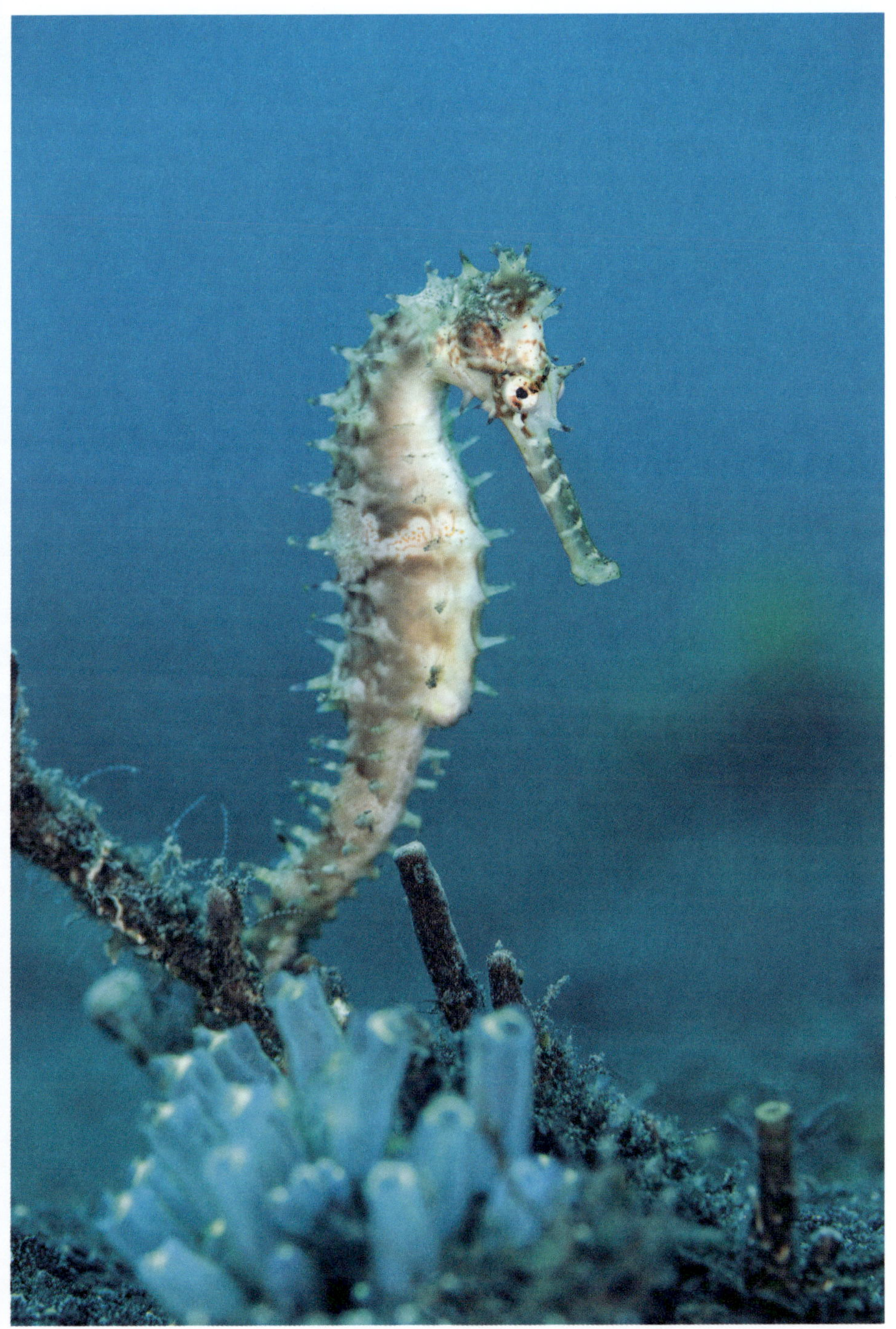

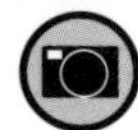
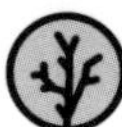
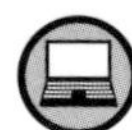

TIPS

- All digital cameras show you a Jpeg as a review image, even if you only shoot Raw files, and that Jpeg can have a lot of processing applied, which makes it hard to judge exposures. For a more accurate review image, set your Picture mode to Standard or Natural.

- This is a quick exercise that can be done at the start of a couple of wideangle dives. Just avoid doing it on a day when the sun is constantly popping in and out of clouds.

WIDEANGLE BLUES

The background of most wideangle photos is the blue of the ocean, and how attractively you capture this blue has a massive impact on the appeal of your images. Many factors control the hue of blue including whether the sun is out, the height of the sun in the sky, and the water clarity, and that's before you get to the camera. Personal preference is also part of the equation, and some shots will look better with blues of different brightness.

Shutter speed is the primary control of blue exposures because it doesn't alter the look of a typical wideangle foreground, which is lit with an instantaneous burst of flash. The aim of this assignment is to spend some time taking full control over your blue and getting to know how your preferred shade of blue should look when you review your shots underwater.

Start by framing up a typical wideangle scene but leave your flashes off. Take a series of identically composed shots with different exposures until you get the blue you think is best and then delete all but that shot. Take a series of three shots, increasing the shutter speed by a third of a stop each time. Return to the original settings and take another series of three shots, this time overexposing by a third of a stop each time. After the dive, download and compare the results to appreciate how much difference a third of a stop makes. If your preferred blue isn't the first shot in the sequence, make a note of how much you need to compensate to get a blue you like.

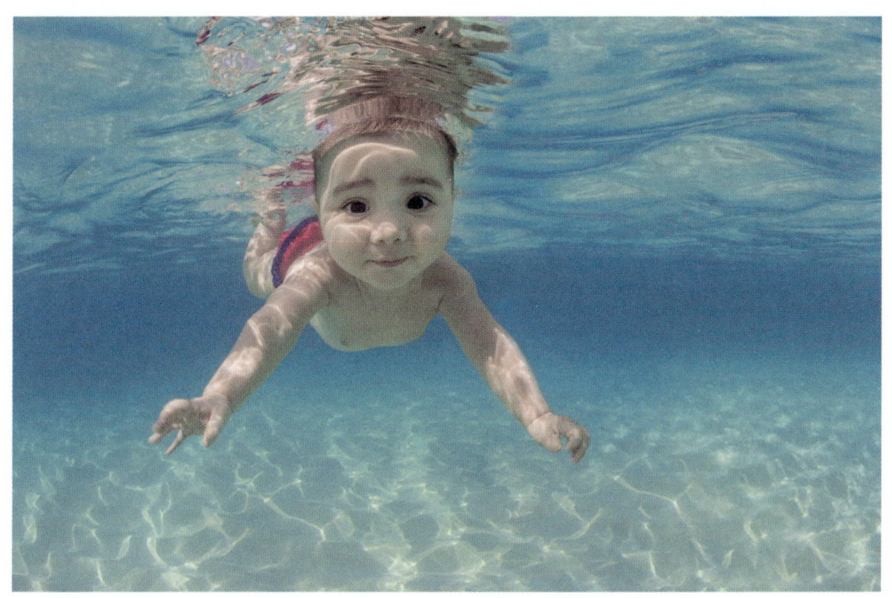

▲ *A longer exposure brightens the water's color, creating a light blue that is spacious and inviting.*

▼ *A shorter exposure creates a darker blue, which creates a moody and mysterious atmosphere.*

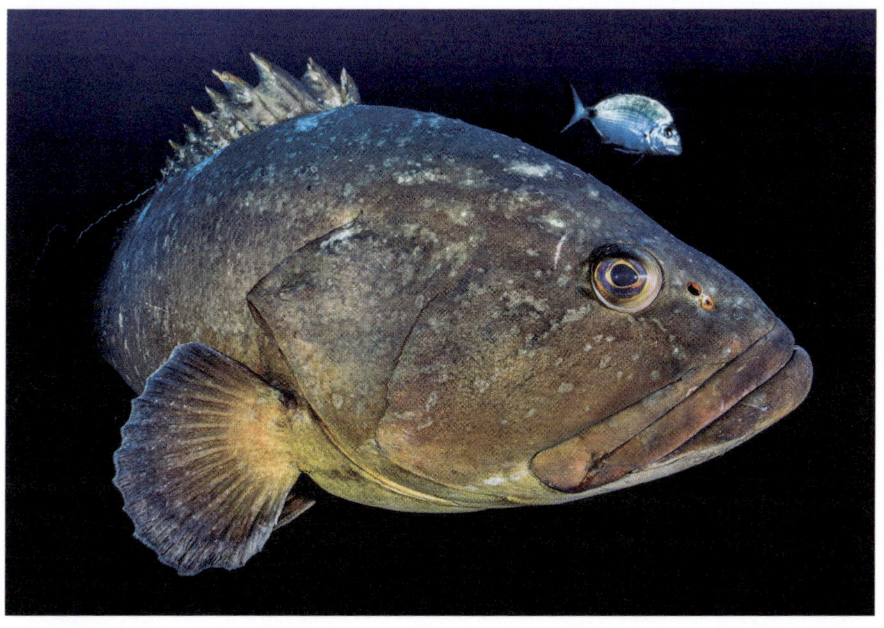

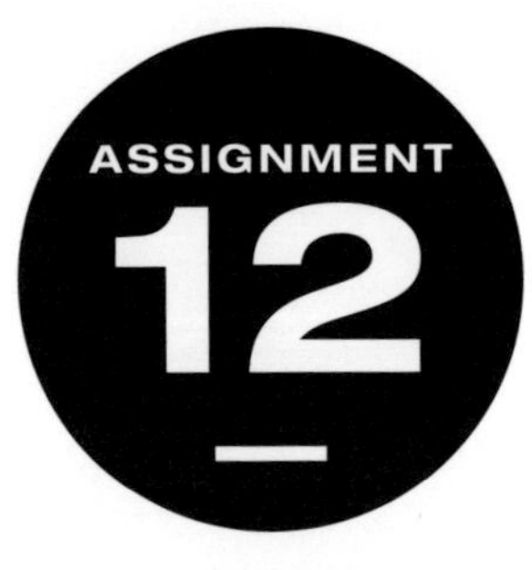

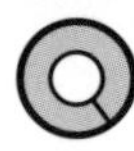

TIPS

- There is no "correct" aperture for depth of field. It varies with subject magnification and lens, and depends entirely on what looks best to you.

- All modern interchangeable-lens cameras have excellent image quality below ISO 800, so you should adjust your shooting technique accordingly.

▶ *Depth of field is critical to the success of macro pictures. You might choose to have lots or just a little, or even something in between, but it is important to take control of it.*

BOSSING DEPTH OF FIELD

I have another exercise that will help you learn a valuable shortcut made possible by modern cameras. Underwater time is always limited, and efficient techniques are best. I'm sure you know that closing the aperture (selecting a higher f-stop) increases depth of field and vice versa. The catch is that when you open or close the aperture, it doesn't only change depth of field, but also the exposure of both the ambient light and your strobes. For this assignment, I want you to shoot a series of macro images in which you change the aperture for each and accompany it with an opposite adjustment of ISO to maintain a consistent exposure.

You don't need to be a math genius to be a photographer because all the exposure controls on our cameras are in proportion. An equal change of aperture, shutter speed, or ISO all adjust exposure by the same amount. All you need to do is count the clicks and rotate the dials in the right direction. Repeat the assignment regularly to build up muscle memory so this becomes a quick and automatic technique, giving you complete control over the look of your macro images.

The big advantage of this technique is that it allows you to change depth of field without wasting time reaching out and changing strobe powers, something that might also disturb your subject.

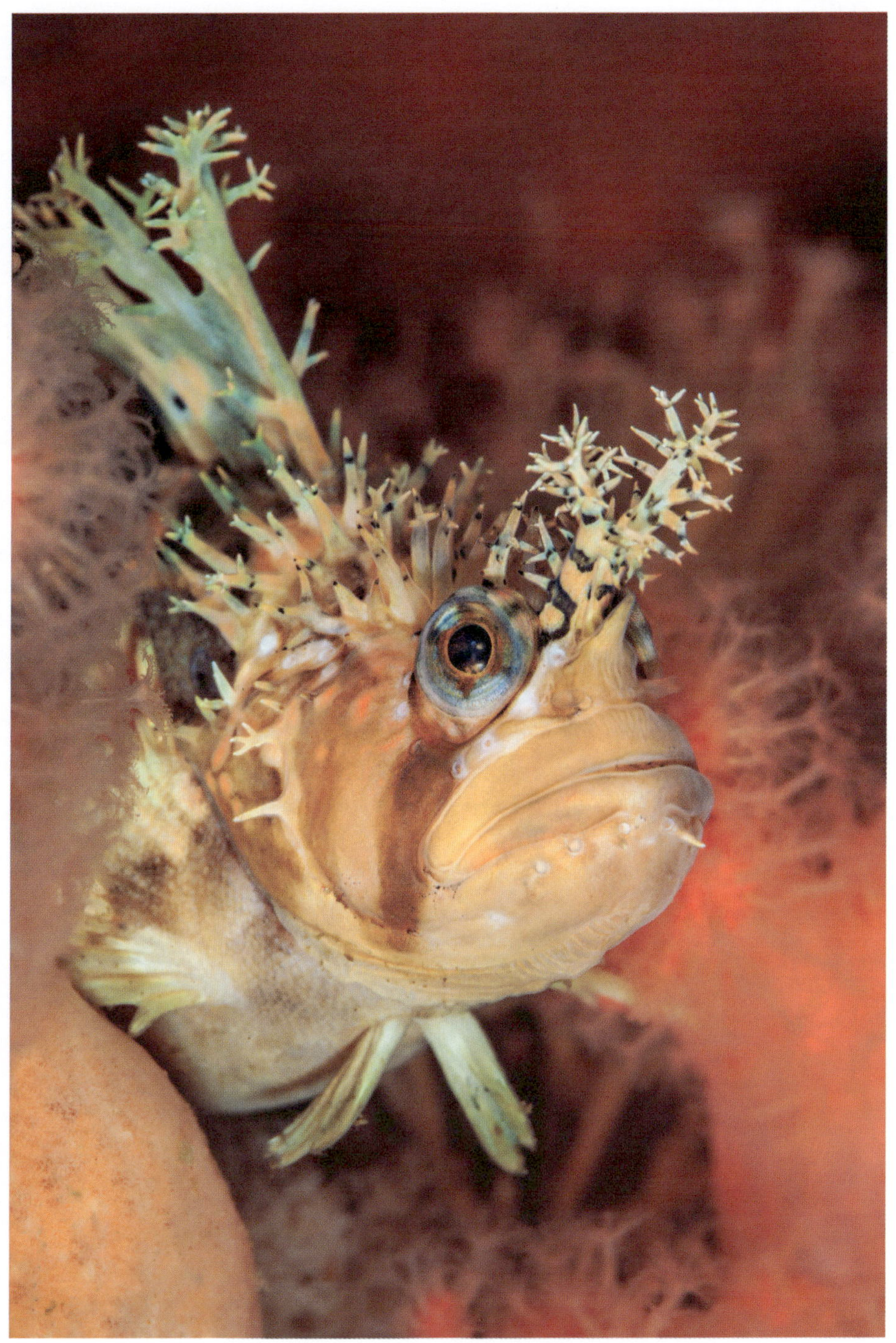

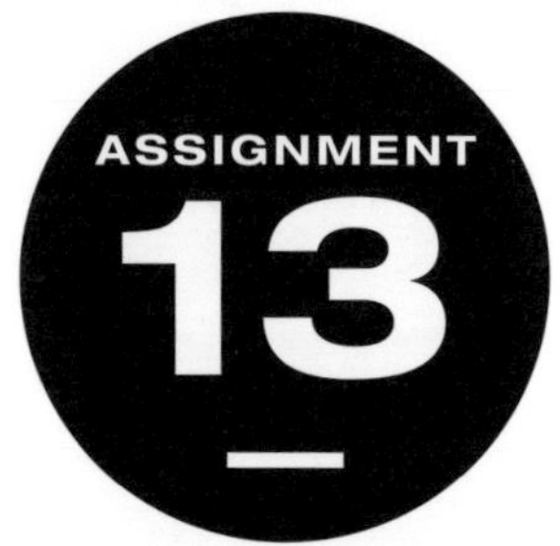

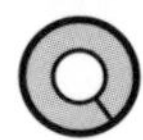
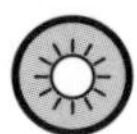

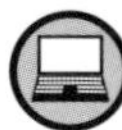

TIPS

- There aren't too many rules for these types of images, other than most of the time patterns look best when everything is in focus. Use a closed aperture such as f/16 and keep the camera parallel to the subject to maximize depth of field.

- Encrusting marine life usually provides the best colors and patterns. The richest encrusting life is usually found in areas of current, and the most colorful species are often in shady spots.

▶ *There is an inexhaustible supply of natural patterns underwater.*

NATURAL PATTERNS

In the days of film, underwater photographers were limited to 36 photos on a dive and would pace their shots to last the dive. Inevitably, we'd save a few frames "just in case," which would be hurriedly exposed as the dive ended. When shooting macro, one of the easiest images to take is a close-up of some interestingly patterned invertebrate life, with the camera parallel to the subject and the aperture closed right down for maximum depth of field.

Every film photographer had a big collection of these natural patterns in their portfolio, but digital cameras have changed the way we shoot and think, and combined with the advances in autofocus, few serious underwater photographers bother to collect these kinds of shots anymore. In this assignment, I want you to get creative and fill this gap in your portfolio.

Look for pleasing symmetry, color combinations, and repetition. Invertebrate life such as sea squirts, bryozoans, corals, sponges, starfish, and sea cucumbers have amazing patterns and details. Fish-scale patterns are often stunning too, most easily photographed when they are sleeping at night, or on dive sites where fish are habituated to divers. Natural patterns are attractive on their own but will really catch the eye when different patterns are shown together. Pick your favorites and create a grid of four or more images in Photoshop.

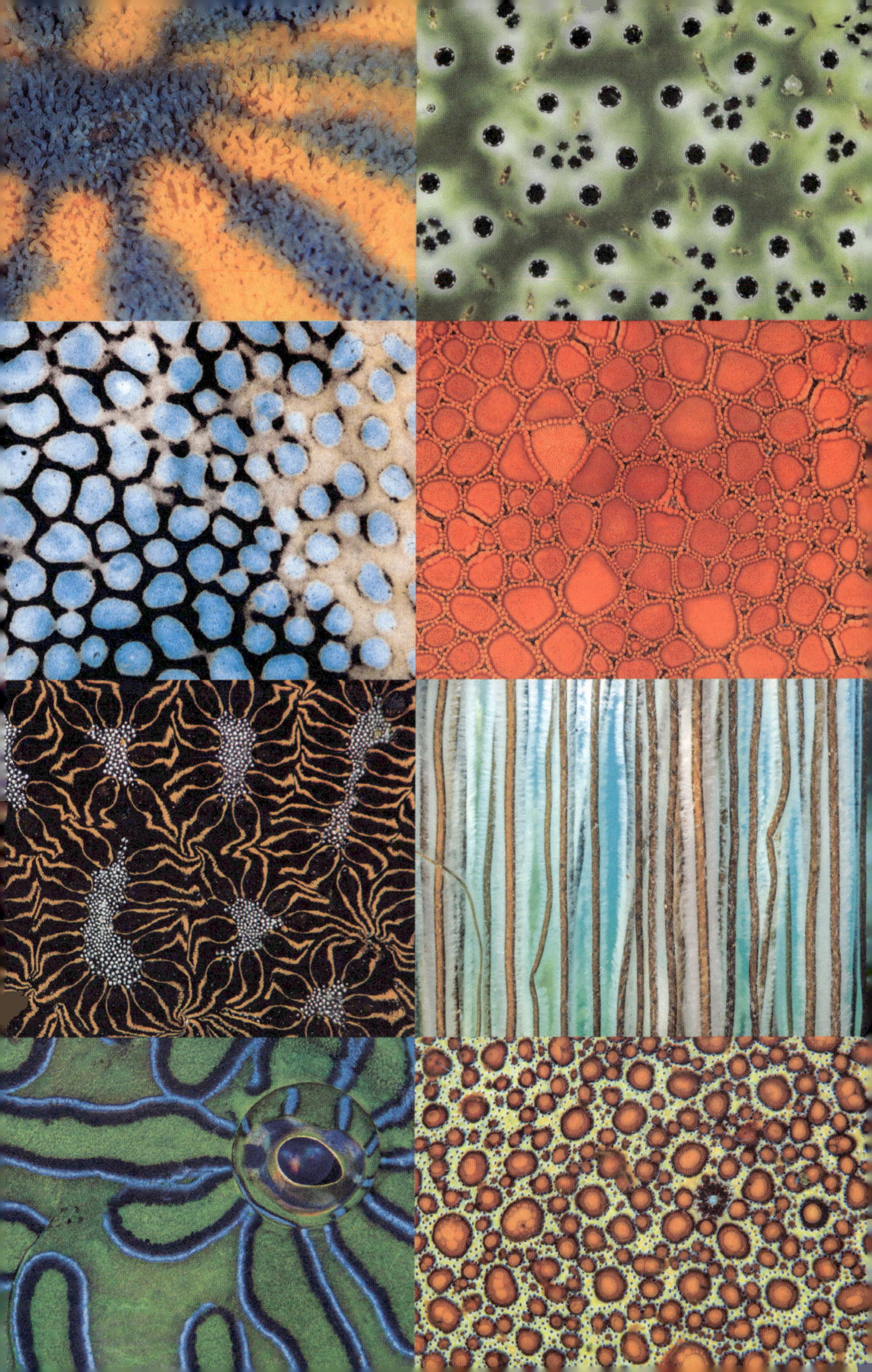

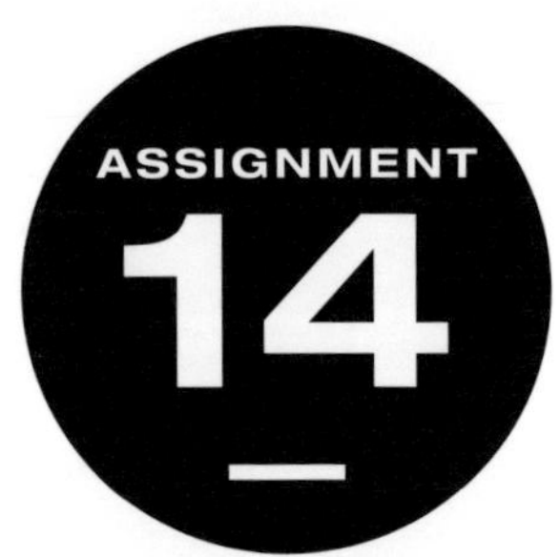

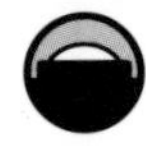
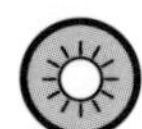
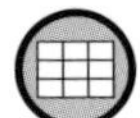

TIPS

- Inward lighting, where you push your strobes out wide and aim them in at the camera, is ideal for these shots, as you will light the subject without spraying strobe light onto the reef behind.

- Try to compose the subject so it is contained within the dark silhouette of the reef, while still having plenty of blue water in the frame beyond to create depth.

- A zoom lens helps you control the relative size of foreground and background elements in wideangle shots. If the background is too small, back away slightly and zoom in. The subject will stay the same size, but the background will grow.

BANG WITH BLACK

Rich colors invariably look their most impressive when isolated against a black background. The aim of this assignment is to exploit this idea, which is commonly used for macro, when shooting wideangle scenery. The goal is to frame a colorful subject, such as a red soft coral, yellow sponge, or orange sea fan, against a black background created by a distant silhouetted reef, so the color jumps out of the picture.

Don't simply speed up the shutter until the water goes dark, as you also want some attractive blue water in the frame. Instead, these pictures are made possible by understanding the ambient light and identifying the right subject. To get a silhouetted reef wall, you need to dive on the shady side of the reef, which is usually where more colorful sponges and soft corals will be growing. Descend the wall, so there is at least 15ft (5m) of reef above you—this will provide the backdrop. You then need to find a subject that is in the shade but also sticks out from the reef. Being in the shade lets you frame it against the silhouetted reef without the sun coming into the shot, and because it sticks out, it will be easy to isolate with strobe light.

Once you have the settings and lighting dialed in, shoot a series of similar subjects using the same technique. This is always a much more efficient way to work underwater, making better use of your time than reconfiguring the camera and settings for every subject.

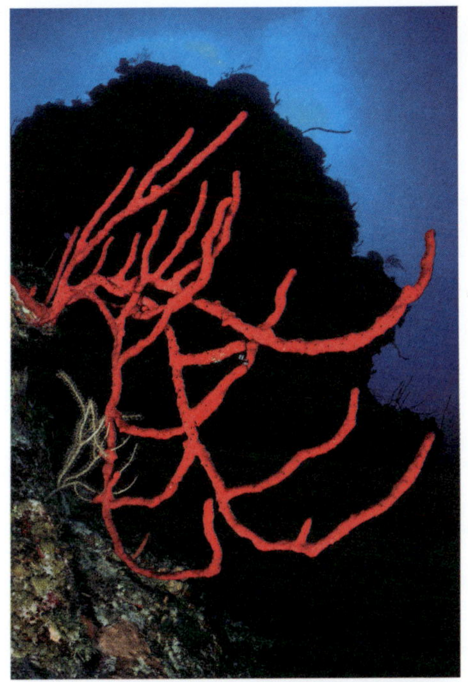

► Find a colorful subject in the shade to frame against the black of the reef.

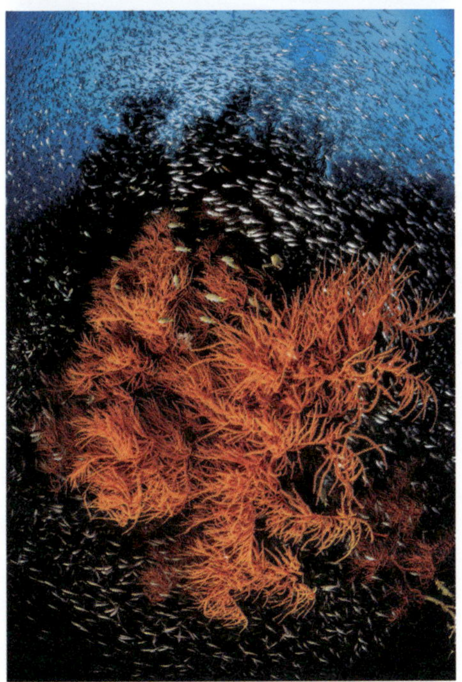

◄ This is a technique to use time and again, even in bustling scenes, as placing color against black makes it pop.

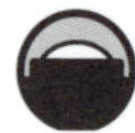
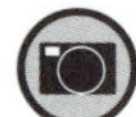

TIPS

- Because the camera is so close to the subject, WAM images have limited depth of field. Shut down the aperture to compensate, using a higher ISO to help get enough ambient light into the shots.

- Strobes need to be positioned very tight to the end of the lens to light the front of the subject. They will likely be on very low power because they are so close.

▼ *This thumb-sized frogfish appears as a mighty predator thanks to WAM.*

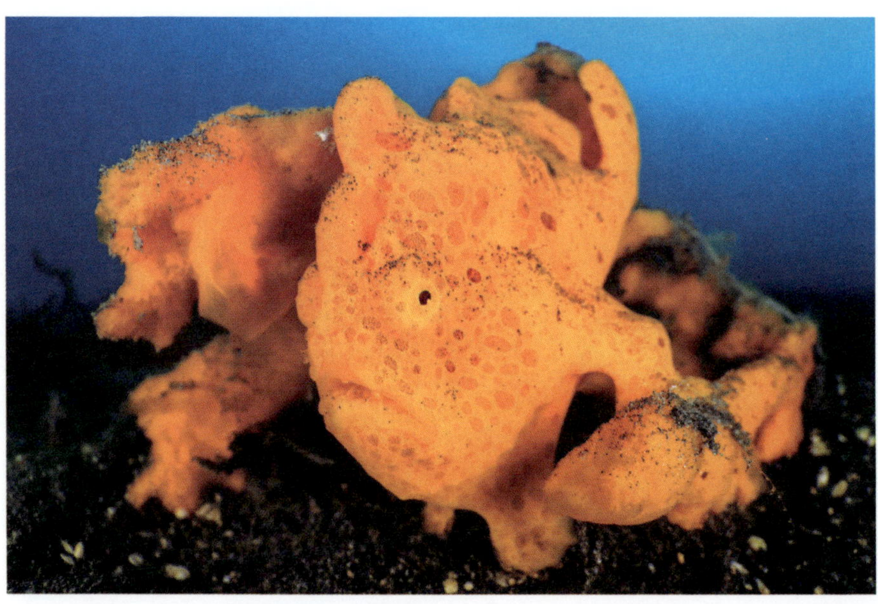

WIDEANGLE MACRO

Wideangle macro (WAM) can create some of the most dramatic underwater images. It is an extreme form of close-focus wideangle, where the camera is optimized for extreme close-up shooting, while still using a wideangle lens. WAM bestows macro subjects with big animal charisma, revealing them with macro-like magnifications against a wideangle background. This technique is highly suited to underwater photography and the last few years have seen exciting advances in camera equipment, allowing us to push the boundaries even further.

There is a lot of WAM gear available, but this is a technique all about extremes, so the more cutting edge the optic, the more dramatic your pictures. If you are using a fisheye lens, the smaller your dome port, the closer you can get it and the larger the subject will appear. Nauticam's EMWL lens system is the ultimate WAM tool, but I don't recommend committing to such a cost until you've fallen for this technique.

The first step is identifying and finding suitable subjects—you need confident creatures that can be approached closely, such as frogfish, moray eels, anemonefish, or scorpionfish. Next, you need to dial in your lighting and exposure, which is best done away from the subject. Strobes need to be set to low power and ISO and shutter speed should be adjusted to allow ambient light into the frame. Once on the subject, slowly work closer and closer, making the pictures increasingly impactful. Where possible, include background elements, so the picture is about more than the subject.

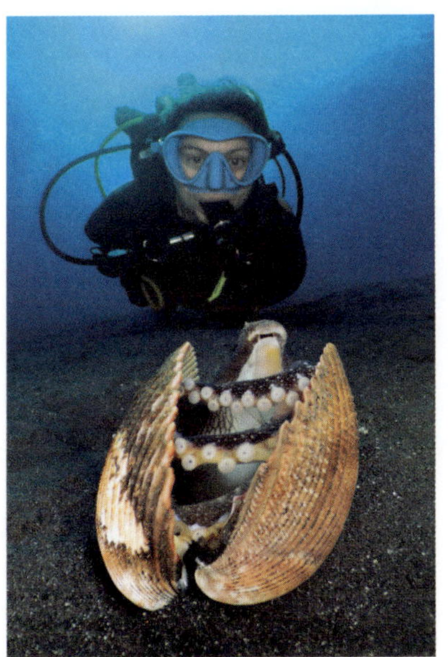

PRO TIPS

- Focus on wideangle macro images when it is sunny and bright, as the extra light makes it easier to expose the background of the images.

- WAM involves positioning the camera close to subjects. Practice the technique on rocks and set up your lighting away from the subject, so you don't scare the wildlife while shooting.

◀ *Coconut octopus are small enough to fit into clam shells, but WAM makes them look an impressive size.*

ASSIGNMENT 16

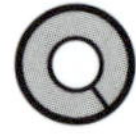 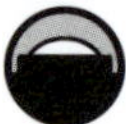
 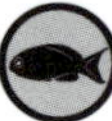

TIPS

- Mechanical lenses don't focus automatically. The best approach is to focus them until approximately correct and then make the final adjustments by slowly moving the camera in and out until the subject is in focus.

- Shooting with an open aperture often means you have too much light. If your system can do HSS (see Assignment 43), use this. Alternatively, use a 2- or 3-stop neutral density (ND) filter on the lens.

- Backgrounds should be your focus for the vintage lens assignment. Some photographers take shiny artificial backgrounds, like steel wool, which create highlights that expand into blobs. Personally, I prefer the challenge of finding suitable backgrounds in nature.

▼ *The sparkling background behind this orange anthias is actually a school of silvery glassfish. That said, artificial backgrounds are an ideal way to practice this technique but view them as a teaching aid.*

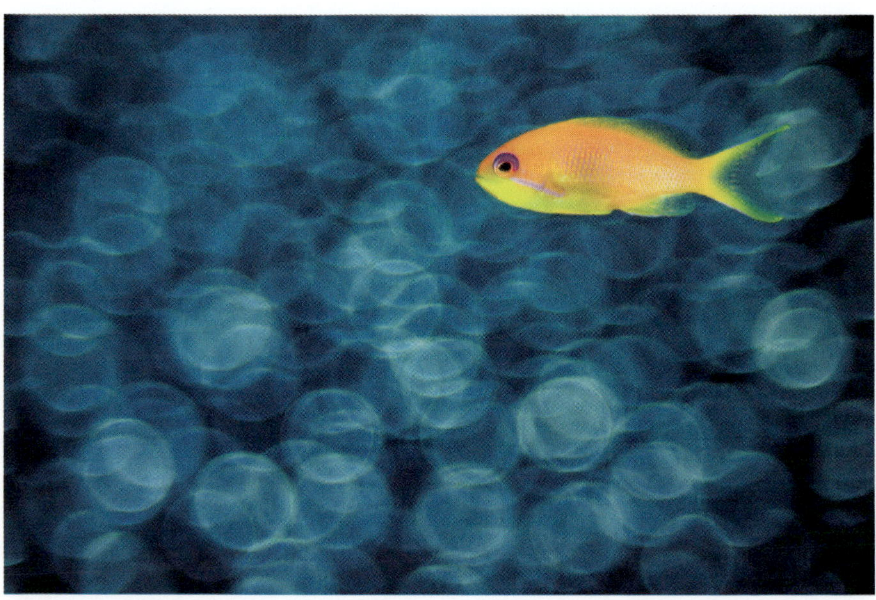

VINTAGE LENSES

Modern lenses are high quality and work automatically with your camera to help you get great shots. Your challenge for this assignment is to try an old, manual-focus vintage lens underwater. The most popular vintage lenses are macro and portrait lenses between 50mm and 100mm, which can be used in conjunction with extension tubes or close-up lenses to enable them to focus close enough for underwater shooting. The attraction of these lenses is in using them with an open aperture, because their simple construction creates a distinctive and attractive bokeh from out-of-focus backgrounds. Although the perspective is similar to your existing macro lenses, the look of the images is totally different.

There are many lenses to choose from, and there is no need to follow the herd. Most photographers plump for lenses they have seen others using, so fashionable optics quickly become overpriced, while others that create just as interesting images sell for pocket money. There are even some modern recreations of vintage lenses on the market, such as the reasonably priced TTArtisan 100mm f/2.8 prime. All can easily be fitted to almost any camera with an inexpensive mechanical adaptor. Vintage lenses tend to be fully manual, so you have to set the aperture (fully open) before diving and focus manually using a gear.

Key to this assignment is finding subject matter that looks great out of focus. I usually search for such backgrounds first and then photograph whatever is around as the focal point. Backgrounds with pinpricks of brightness usually work best because these expand into bokeh blobs when out of focus. Aim for compositions with a sharp subject set against attractive, abstract surroundings.

PRO TIPS

- Focus peaking on mirrorless cameras is helpful when using a vintage macro or portrait lens, greatly helping you determine when the eyes of the subject are precisely in focus.

- The Nikonos 15mm is a different style of vintage lens. Fully manual, but with fantastic optics that beat most modern lenses, they can be found cheaply and with adaptors can be used on modern mirrorless cameras. As it was designed for underwater use, its optics remain impressive, although with a field of view of only 90°, it is not especially wide.

- Using a manual lens slows down your entire photographic process, but many photographers find this a refreshing change from their usual way of shooting—while they shoot fewer frames than with modern lenses, they are happy with a higher percentage. Focus peaking doesn't work well with wideangle lenses, so with Nikonos lenses I magnify my viewfinder and zoom in when reviewing to be sure of critical focus before shooting a sequence.

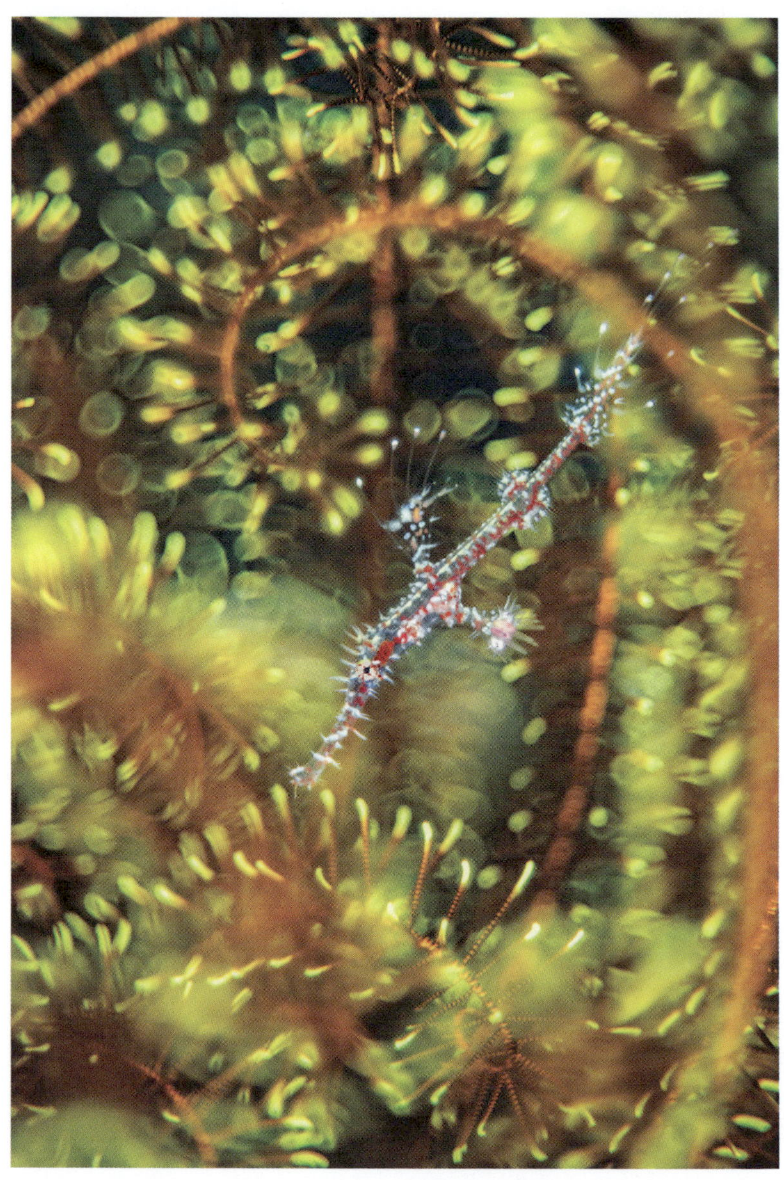

▲ *Vintage lenses are harder to use and not always as sharp as modern lenses but produce interestingly different results. This image was a category winner in the Wildlife Photographer of the Year competition.*

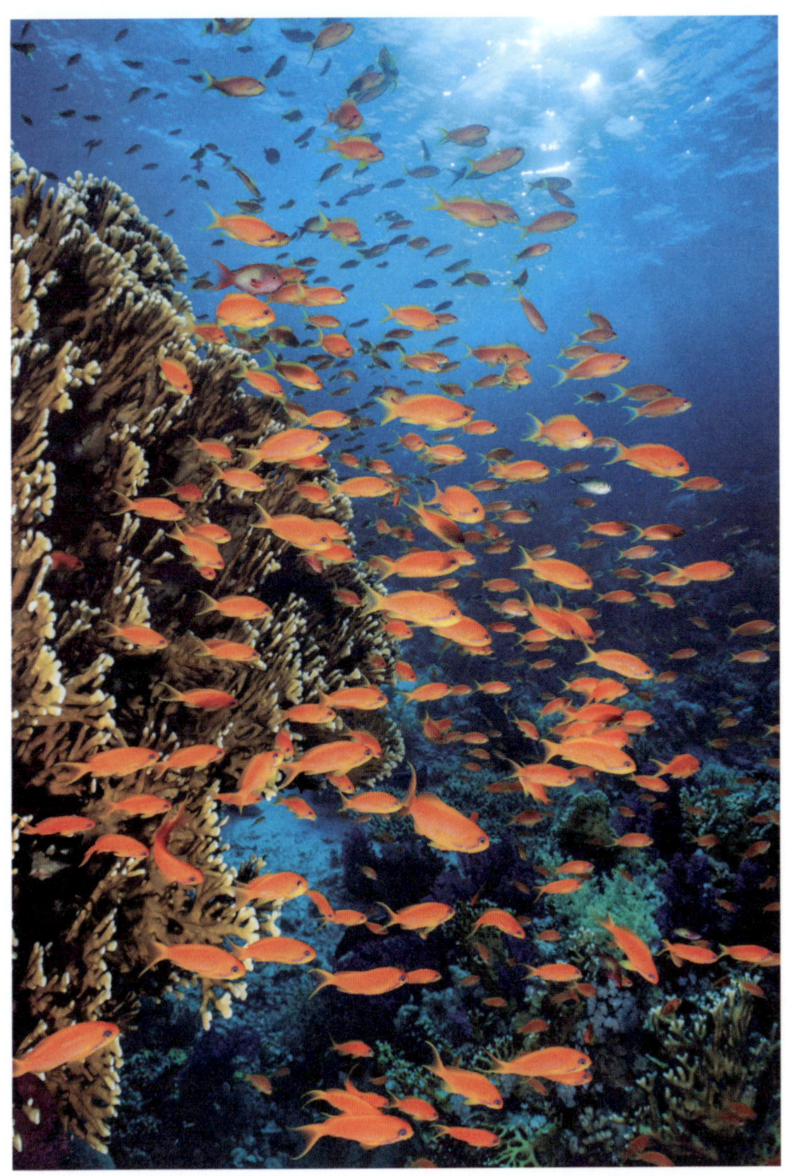

▲ *An alternative is using the fully mechanical Nikonos lenses, such as the 15mm wideangle. Care is needed when setting the focus, but they are excellent underwater optics.*

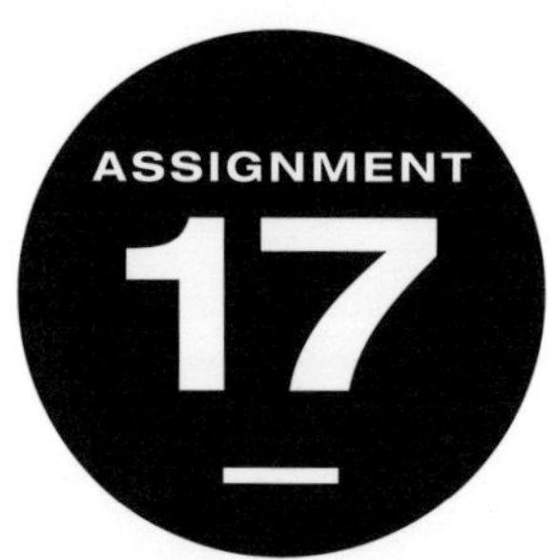

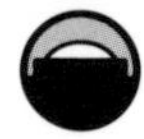
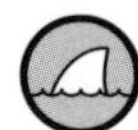
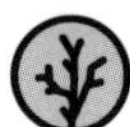
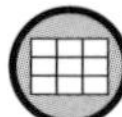

TIPS

- Lighting circular fisheye lenses is similar to working with a standard fisheye. Keep your strobes pulled well back to help the light soften and spread. I ensure mine are behind the line of the back of the housing.

- Circular fisheyes see very wide in all directions. It is very easy to get unwanted elements in the frame, such as your shadow, your fins, your bubbles, and even your fingers on the camera's shutter. Get used to scanning the edges of the composition for UFOs before shooting.

CIRCULAR FISHEYE

Circular fisheye lenses are gimmicky, but shooting with one is a valuable reset button for your approach to composition. You will have to think differently about how to arrange the elements within circular pictures, compared to rectangular ones. Such a wide lens is well suited to underwater photography, but it is also unforgiving of mistakes, especially with lighting. For this assignment, you should shoot the circular fisheye both without and with flash.

Nikon and Canon currently make 8-15mm fisheye lenses that project a circular image at the 8mm end of the zoom, which covers 180° in all directions. You will need to remove the lens hood and the shades from your dome port to use one. INON makes the UFL-M150 lens for compact cameras and OM System makes a circular fisheye lens for its popular TG series.

Compositionally, experiment with central subjects and also with curved shapes within the frame, as both suit circles. Spins and spirals are also effective. Try to keep all sides of the composition light—if part of the frame runs to black, it will break the outline of the frame, merging the picture with the border. Circular fisheye lenses are easiest to use when shooting available light and are well suited to photographing big animals, scenery, and wrecks. Measure your success by producing images that you feel work better in that circular frame.

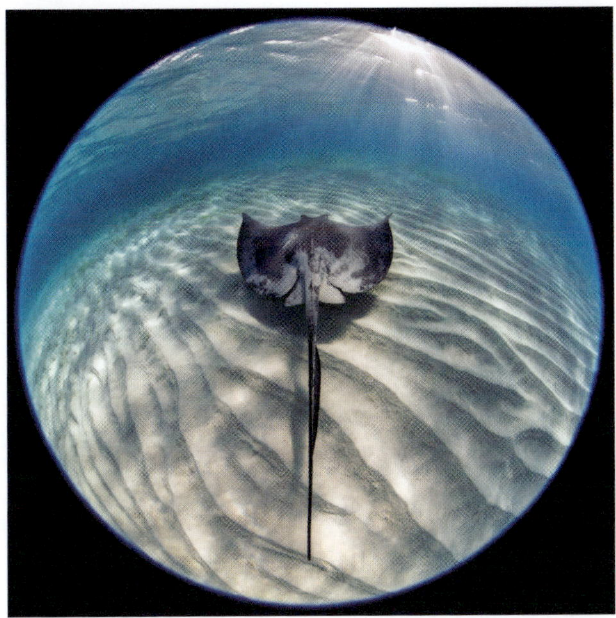

▲ ▼ *Circular frames challenge you to compose elements differently, which is easiest when the frame is mostly illuminated with available light.*

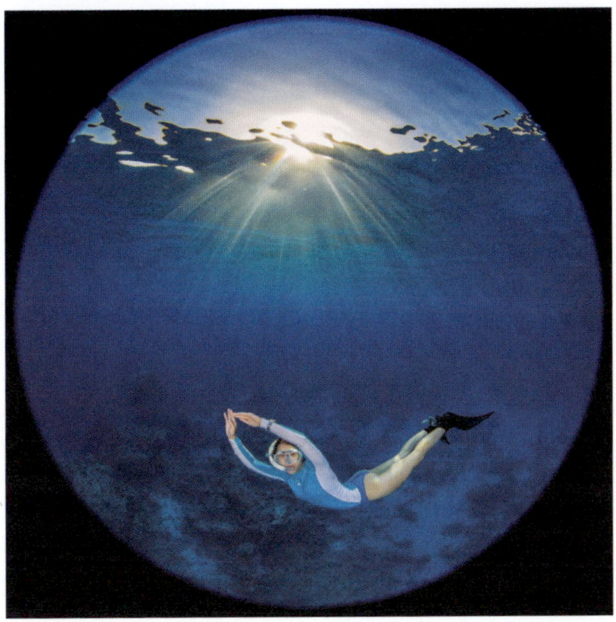

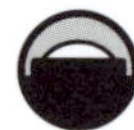 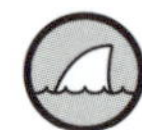
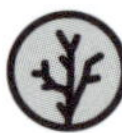 

TIPS

- On full-frame cameras, an aperture between f/20 and f/22 is needed to get everything in focus. On smaller sensors, you can open slightly to f/16-18 and maintain perfect sharpness.

- A 45° viewfinder is ideal for these shots—just remember to take off the rubber part of the eyepiece so that it doesn't collect water and obscure the view.

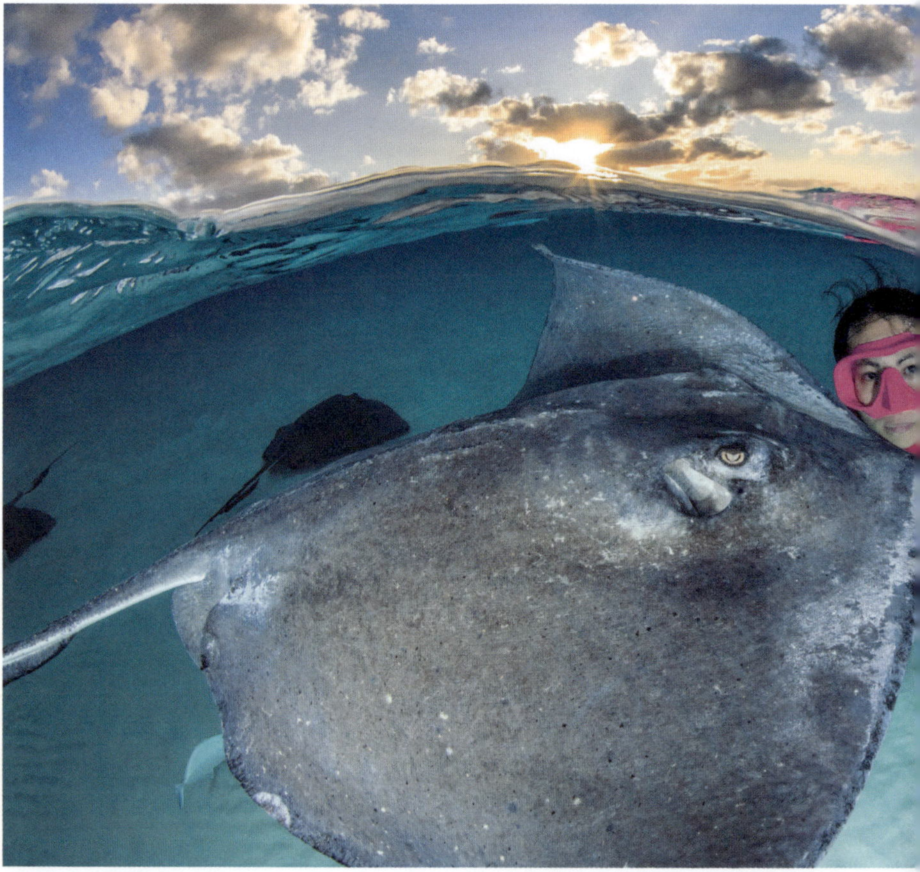

SPLITS WITHOUT A MASK

For this assignment, I want you to shoot split-level shots, but without using a mask, snorkel, or fins. It is a reminder that underwater photography doesn't always mean going scuba or freediving and that you should always keep an open mind about the best way to get the shot. Try this assignment between dives, while at the beach, or even in a local pool, river, or lake.

Planting your feet in the sand makes it very easy to control the water surface and it allows you to focus on using the correct technique to get both halves in focus. Carefully focus on the underwater subject or scenery and then stop the lens down to have enough depth of field to get above-water details sharp. If the sun is out and high in the sky, you don't need to use strobes. I usually rub something on my dome before shooting splits, such as a wedge of raw potato, baby shampoo, or saliva, then let it dry and rinse when I get in, so that the film that remains prevents droplets.

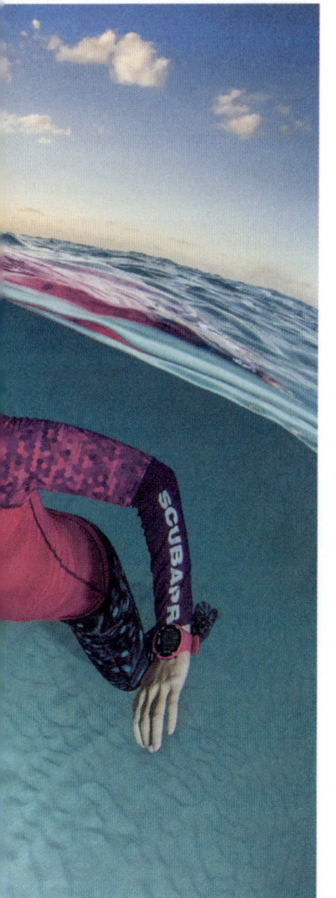

Corals, seaweed, and other marine life in the shallows are great subjects. If the surface is calm, sun patterns also make an attractive scene. Above the surface, palm trees, cliffs, and even buildings will help complete the picture, or ask a buddy to come in and pose. Once you get used to underwater photography without swimming, challenge yourself to get your underwater camera into the most unusual places, such as rock pools and ponds.

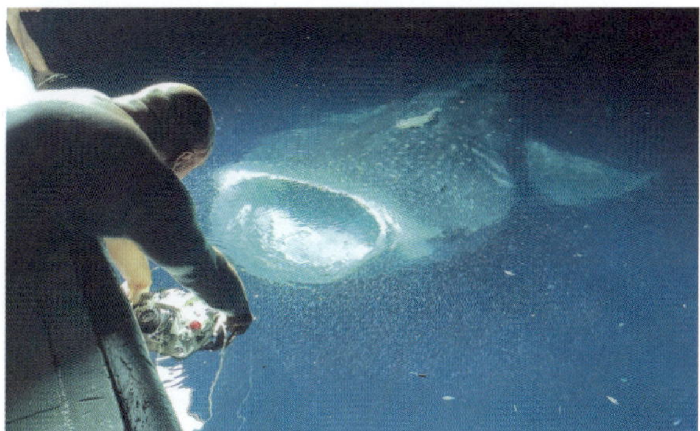

◀ *Split-level shots are fascinating, but you don't need to be fully underwater to shoot them.*

▲ *Remember, you don't need to be swimming or even in the water to take underwater pictures.*

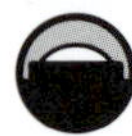

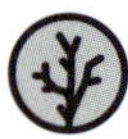

TIPS

- When you spot a good scene, get in position and wait. Your movement will create ripples that will take about 30 seconds to clear. If the breeze picks up, wait for it to drop before shooting.

- Stay shallow and shoot horizontally. Compose with the horizon in the middle of the picture.

- A zoom lens will let you fill more of the frame with a reflection. The wider the lens, the shallower you need to be, otherwise your picture will be dominated by Snell's window (see Assignment 20).

▼ *Calm conditions are essential for reflections, so learn to predict them.*

▶ *Colorful subjects close to the surface in dark conditions give spectacular reflections with flash.*

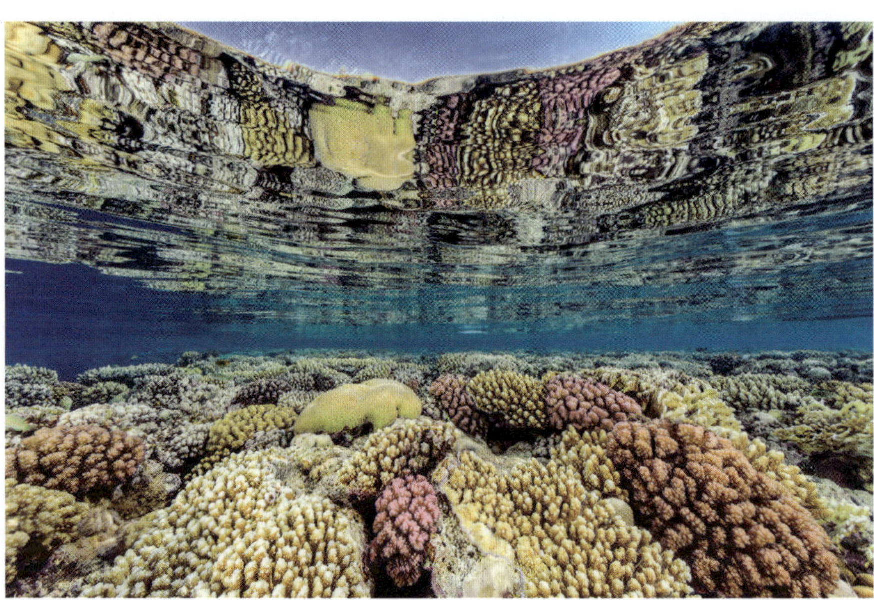

SURFACE REFLECTIONS

This is another assignment that is best done without scuba. The best reflections come from the smoothest water, and breathing through a snorkel keeps the surface flat, while exhaling bubbles will disturb it. Reflections reveal the texture of water and since this is ever-changing, they add an unrepeatable element to your photos. Your task is to shoot reflections using the surface of the water, either as a wideangle shot or as a tighter composition.

Calm water is essential, and it is worth learning how to find it because it makes many types of shots possible, including sun rays and splits. Sheltered bodies of water such as lakes, cenotes, and pools are regularly calm, and windless days naturally bring flat water at sea, but are rarer. Pay attention to prevailing wind direction to predict where there will be shelter, such as in bays or beneath cliffs. Even a large dive boat at anchor will create a photographically exploitable calm. Or when the sea happens to flatten, change your plans and make the most of it.

In bright daylight, reflections are easily shot with just available light, but in dark conditions, you can shoot very dramatic reflections against black water. Where seaweed or corals grow up to the surface, you can shoot attractive closed reflections. A zoom lens is a good choice because it allows you to precisely frame reflections and create a variety of shots. For this assignment, I'd encourage you to produce a range of shots and try both bright conditions and black-water shots.

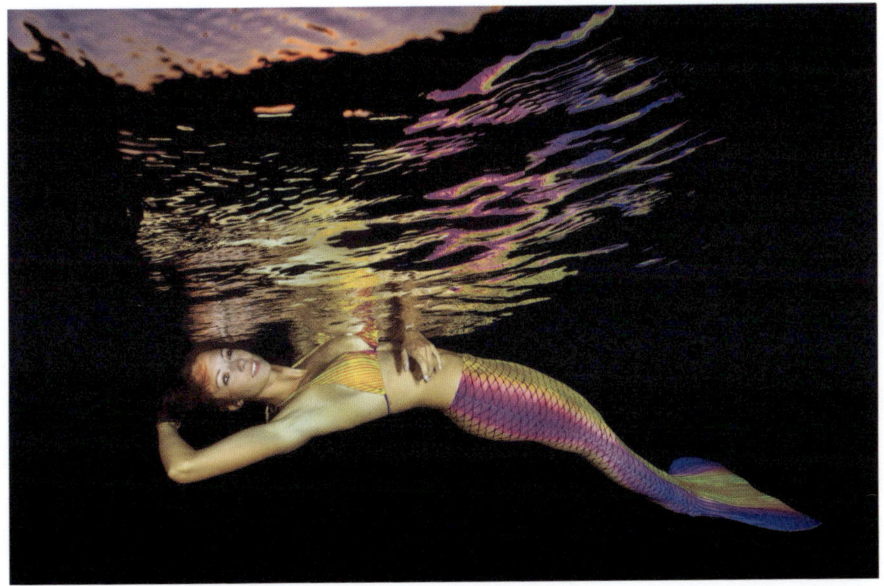

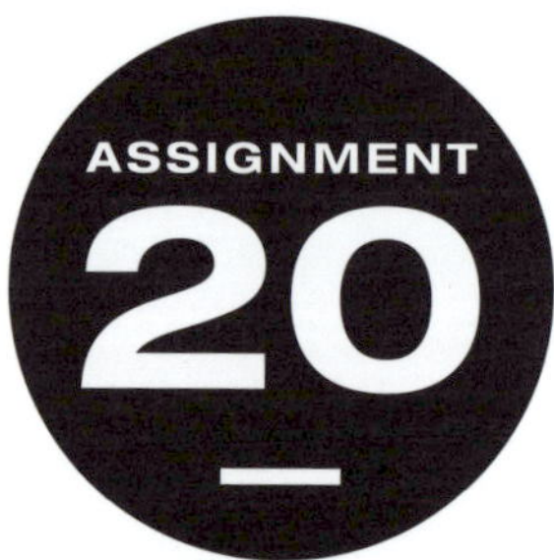

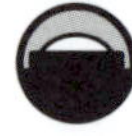

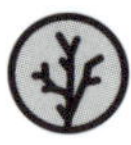

TIPS

- You can only photograph a complete Snell circle with a circular fisheye (see Assignment 17), but the partial circles recorded by other types of lenses are still very attractive.

- In shallow water, we can incorporate above-water elements into our pictures by shooting up through the window.

- When there is a big exposure difference across the window, you should expose for the sky and let the reflected water turn dark.

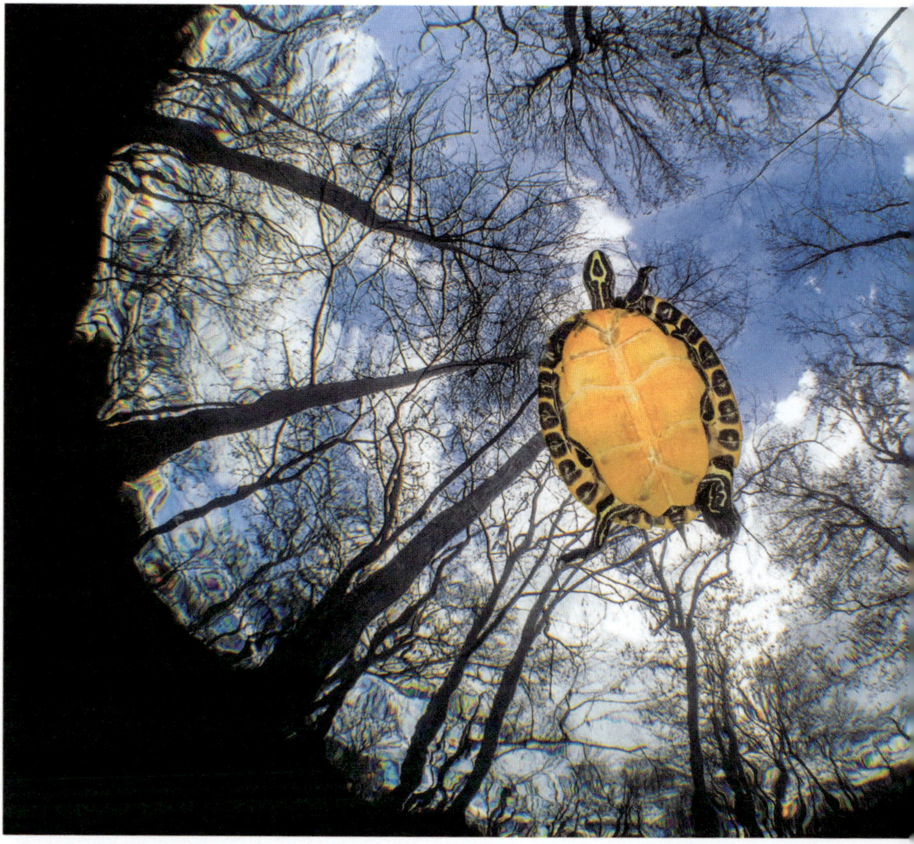

SNELL'S WINDOW

Snell's window is created by the curved boundary between reflected light and refracted light as you look up at the surface. You don't really notice it as a diver, but the moment you point an ultra-wideangle lens upward, it is unmissable. The window is circular, with the reflected underwater world creating a frame surrounding the refracted view through to the sky. The wider your lens, the more the camera can see.

The arc of Snell's window is one of the commonest background elements that you can incorporate in wideangle shots. This assignment isn't designed for a single dive. Instead, I want you to shoot Snell whenever you get the chance from a range of depths and in a range of surface conditions, different weather, and times of day, and store them in a Lightroom collection. The intention of this exercise is to get on first-name terms with Snell's window, so that you build up a quick reference. This will let you predict how Snell will look before entering the water and help you better plan future wideangle pictures.

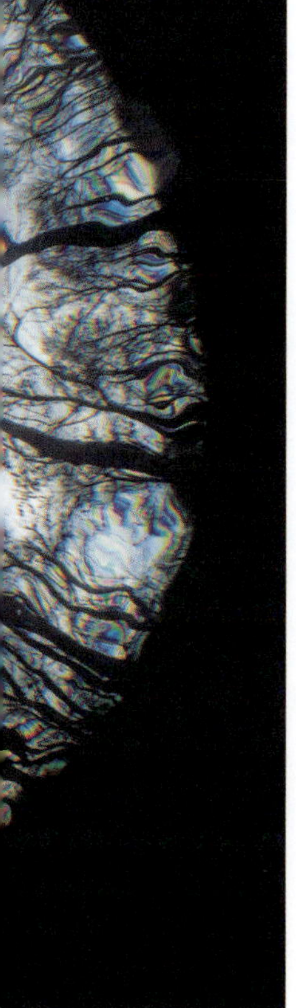

Snell's window is most obvious when the exposure difference between the sky and sea is greatest. This is caused when the sun is low or it is cloudy. Descending deeper reduces the exposure difference. Calm conditions give a sharp boundary, while waves add texture. Snell's window can look great in all forms and adds depth and interest to wideangle pictures. In this assignment, you should use it to frame a subject and as a background element in compositions.

◀ *With low sun, Snell's window is clearly defined and acts as a graphic frame for a freshwater turtle.*

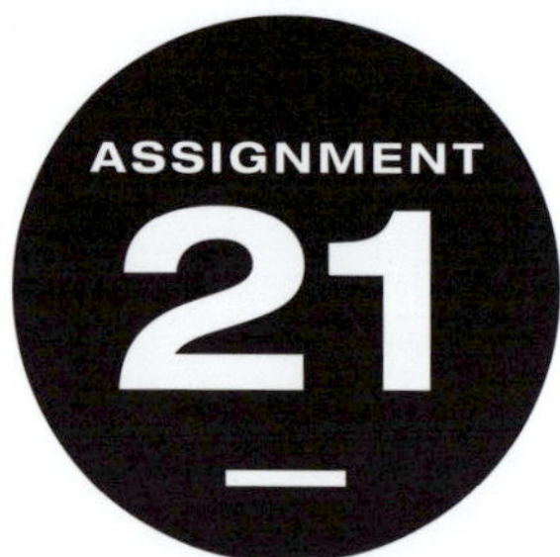

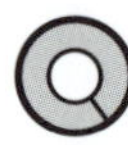
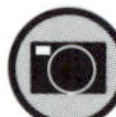
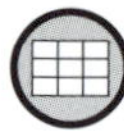

TIPS

- The best way to help your camera to focus isn't some secret autofocus mode but holding it still. A stable camera is an able camera when it comes to focusing.

- Single-point autofocus, where you can move the point, is the best option for this assignment. Try it with and without dynamic tracking to see which you prefer.

▼ *Move your focus point so that the subject is balanced in the picture.*

▶ *A standard opportunity is made more interesting by unusual subject placement.*

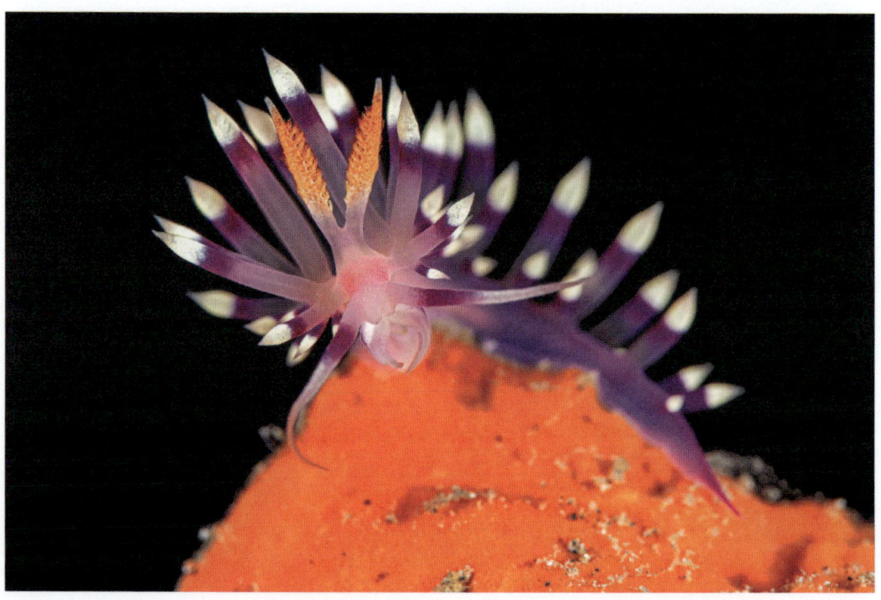

MISSING THE BULLSEYE

The underwater world is a tough place to shoot, and it is easy to slip into the habit of defaulting to the central autofocus point and using it like an aiming sight, shooting every subject in the bullseye. The aim of this assignment is to break that bad habit.

Your challenge is to make an entire macro dive without ever using the central autofocus point. Enjoy exploring the frame and creating different compositions, especially if you are shooting with a mirrorless camera, which typically have autofocus points across the entire frame. As you review the images, make a mental note of the compositions that work for you and start your future macro dives with your autofocus point in this position, rather than the middle.

I never teach that one autofocus mode is better than another, because they all exist for a reason—they can all be exactly the right tool in a certain situation for a certain photographer. Autofocus is there to help, and if a mode isn't helping you then it is the wrong mode, even if someone else—including me—told you they love it.

Part two of this assignment is to dedicate a macro dive not to shooting, but to trying three or four different autofocus modes, using each for 10 to 15 minutes on a range of common subjects. Hopefully, this will give you a feel for what modes work with different subjects and leave you much better placed to catch the action and produce elegant compositions in the future.

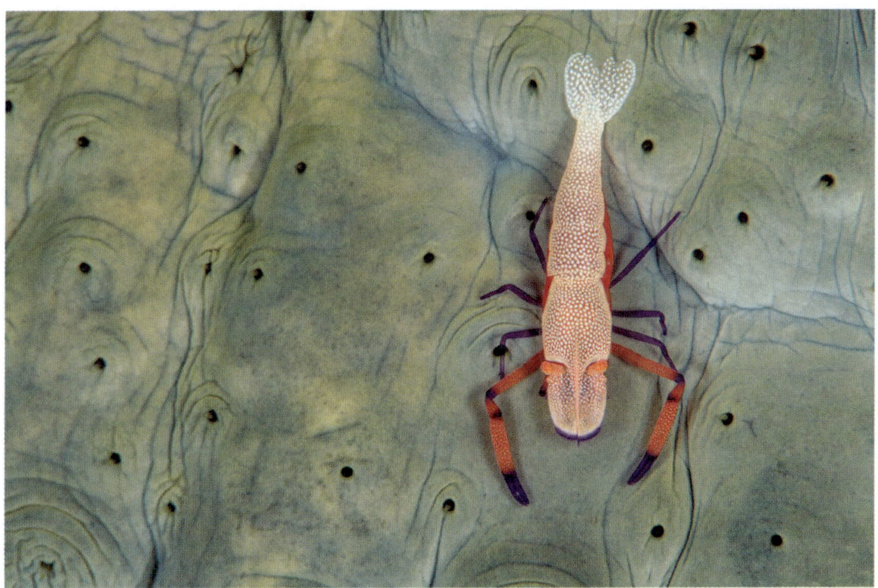

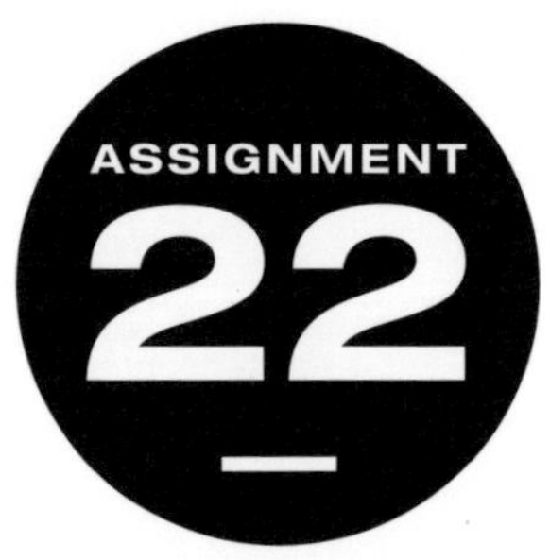

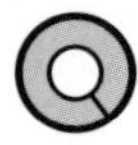

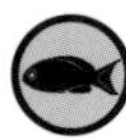

TIPS

- Choose your best-focusing macro lens for this shoot. Shorter focal-length lenses typically focus better than longer lenses, and while you can always crop a mandarinfish shot, you can't refocus once the shot has been taken.

- Mandarinfish usually swim into any current as they spawn. If you want them facing the camera, position yourself up current. If you want them partly side-on, move around about 45º. Don't come around too far or they will swim away from you.

MANDARINFISH

This assignment is focused on shooting the spawning behavior of one species—the colorful mandarinfish. Mandarins live in shallow water on rubbly reefs in the Coral Triangle and many dive resorts in the region run dusk dives to see them. The show starts with the larger males showing off to the females and occasionally fighting with other males in adjacent territories. The male then takes it in turn to spawn with several different females, the pairs making slow spawning rises lasting about five seconds, releasing and fertilizing eggs at the top before darting back to the reef.

Mandarinfish are a unique photographic challenge because the quick action in fading light means you need to think quickly, particularly regarding focusing and backgrounds. At the start of most mandarin dives, there is enough natural light for autofocus to work effectively, although most cameras find it easier if you restrict the focus to a small area of the frame.

As the sun sets fast in the tropics, the light levels will soon get too dark for autofocus. At this point, you should use your focusing light, but set it to a low intensity and use the red-light mode. Mandarinfish don't like light, so I always wait until it is essential to turn it on. Most marine animals are less sensitive to red light, so it works well, but some autofocus systems don't like it either, so if you need white light then use it.

Once the spawning rise starts, with the female perched in the pectoral fin of the male, the fish don't care about much else and this is the time to bring the light onto them, focus, and shoot. Remember, they only release eggs at the top of the rise, so you have a second or two of fluttering fins to get ready for the peak of the action.

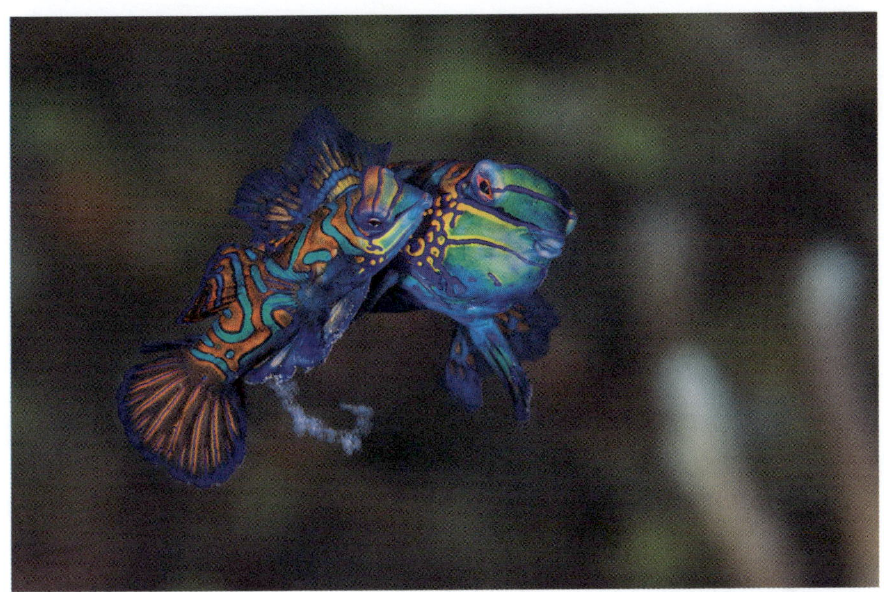

▲ *If the fish are spawning right above the corals, you will need a much more open aperture to blur the distracting reef, so the beautiful fish stand out.*

▼ *If the fish are spawning high above the seabed, get down low and frame them against open water, closing the aperture down to maximize depth of field.*

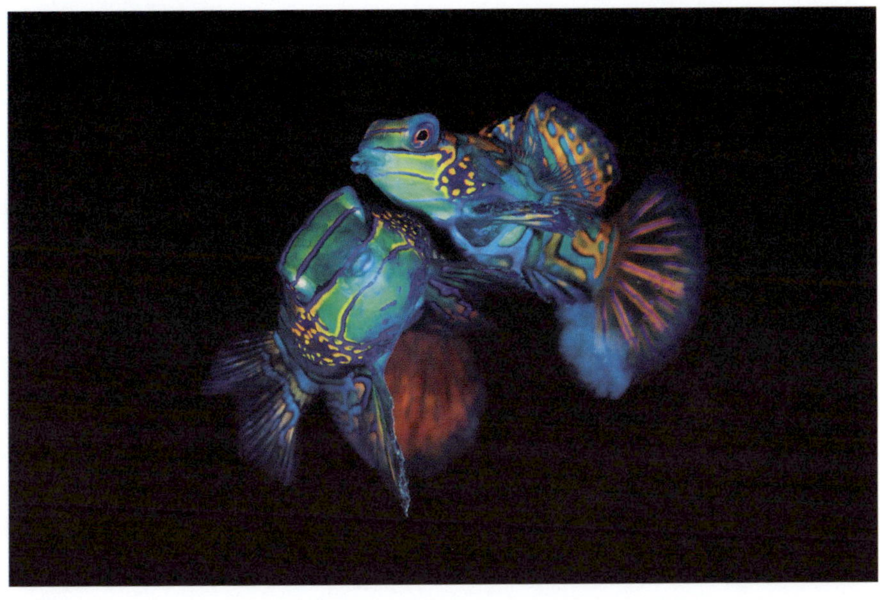

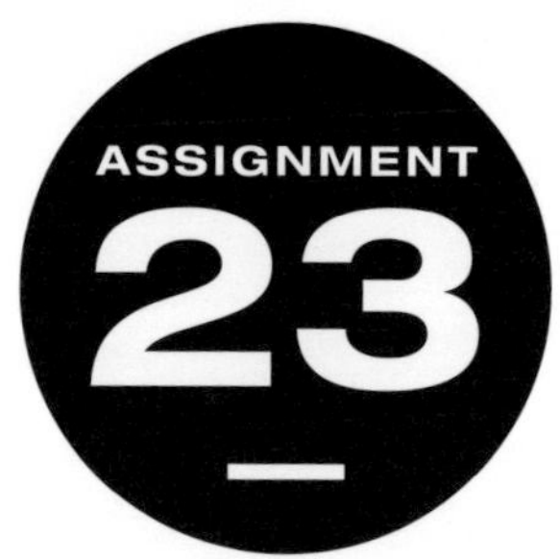

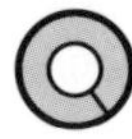

TIPS

- As with mandarinfish (see Assignment 22), focus can be challenging, so select a single autofocus point for the camera to concentrate on.

- I mount my focus light on a ball on the base of my housing, so that its beam is shaded from my eyes when I search for subjects over the top of my housing.

- Additional wideangle lenses, such as a Nauticam MWL on a Flip filter holder, will allow you to quickly take on larger subjects, such as big jellyfish or a blanket octopus, if they appear.

BLACKWATER

Blackwater is a type of night dive conducted in open water. A downline is hung from a buoy and bright lights are attached to it, which draw in the plankton. Divers slowly circulate around the line, checking out every sparkle in their flashlight, hoping it might be a pelagic octopus, larval crustacean, or juvenile fish with outrageous adaptations to living in open water. The downline might drift miles during the dive, but since you drift with it, there is no feeling of current at all. These are very relaxing dives, where you feel like you are suspended in a thick soup of life, rather than diving in open water. By taking on blackwater for this assignment, you are guaranteed to expand your portfolio with images of otherworldly life.

Blackwater photography techniques are straightforward in theory, but much more challenging in practice. The difficulty is getting tiny, semi-translucent, swimming creatures in the frame and in focus, when both you and your subject are adrift in a dark ocean. More than photographic skill, this assignment will demonstrate how important your diving skills are.

Shorter focal-length macro lenses are favored for blackwater because they focus fast and close. Also, ensure that your camera rig is neutrally buoyant for these dives, as this will help your framing and focusing. I use a second handheld spotting flashlight attached to a lanyard for finding subjects. Blackwater is very addictive partly because the more you do it, the more great subjects you will see. And the better the subjects, the better the shots.

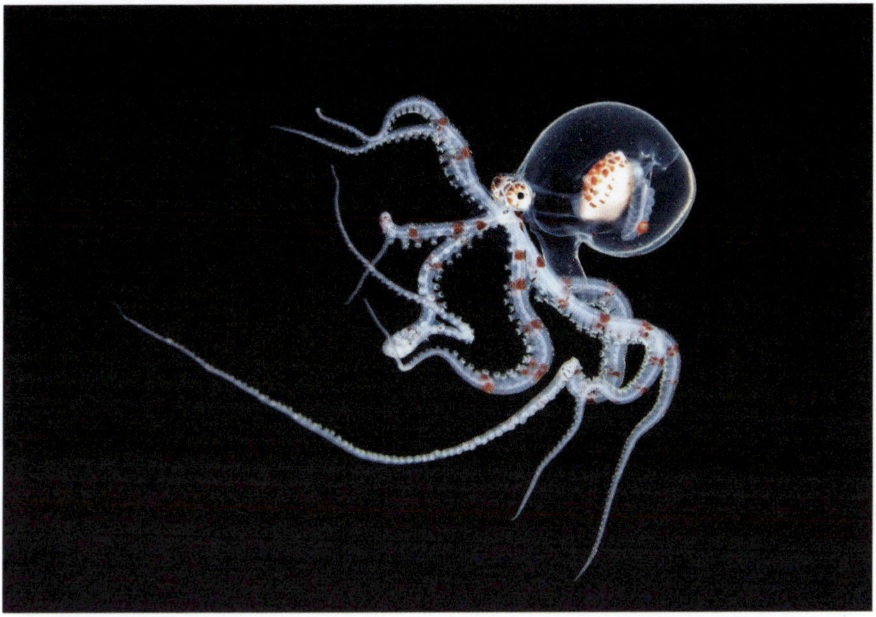

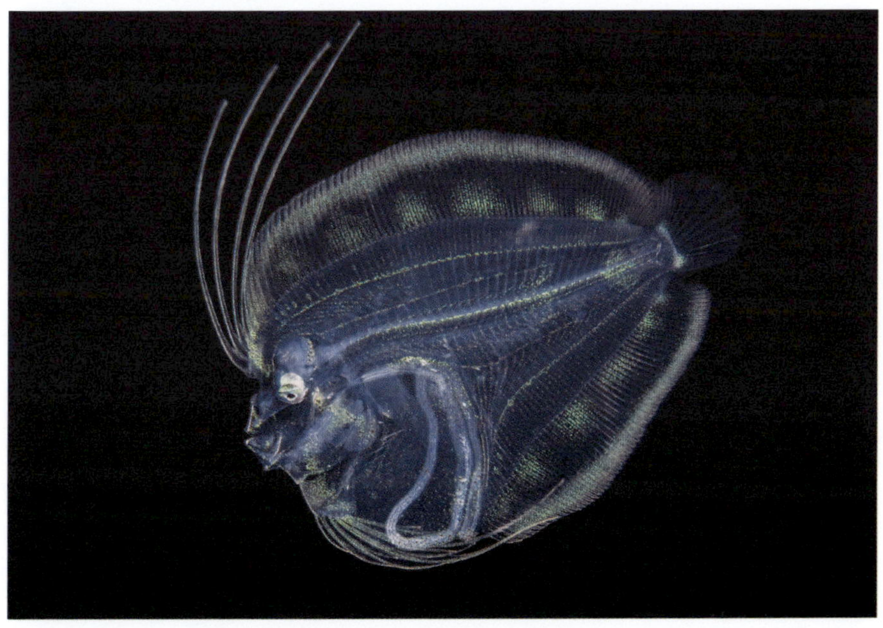

▲ With moving creatures, time your shots carefully for interesting poses.

▼ Don't just spray and pray—make sure the subject is in focus before shooting.

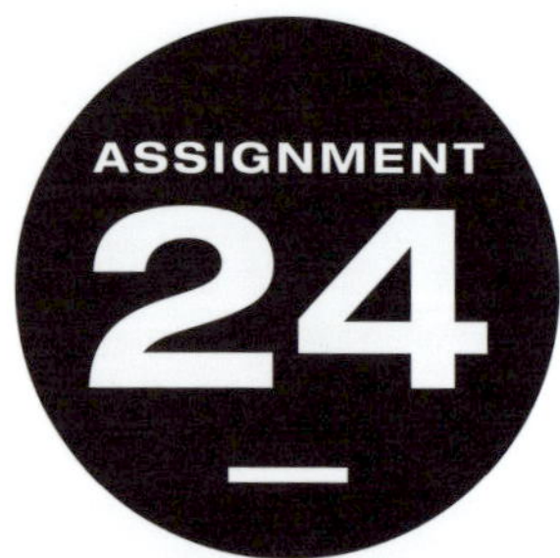

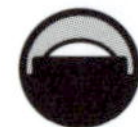
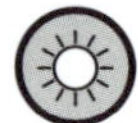

TIPS

- Stay super-shallow for dappled light. If you are at the safety stop depth, you are probably too deep.

- Look for foreground subjects that are just in the shadow of the reef, boat, etc. When you frame them, the composition will have perfect beams and no sun ball.

▼ *The striking beams of light from underwater sunbursts add atmosphere and beauty to your images.*

▶ *Sunbursts are best in the shallows, so if you are not getting good sunbursts, question how deep you are diving.*

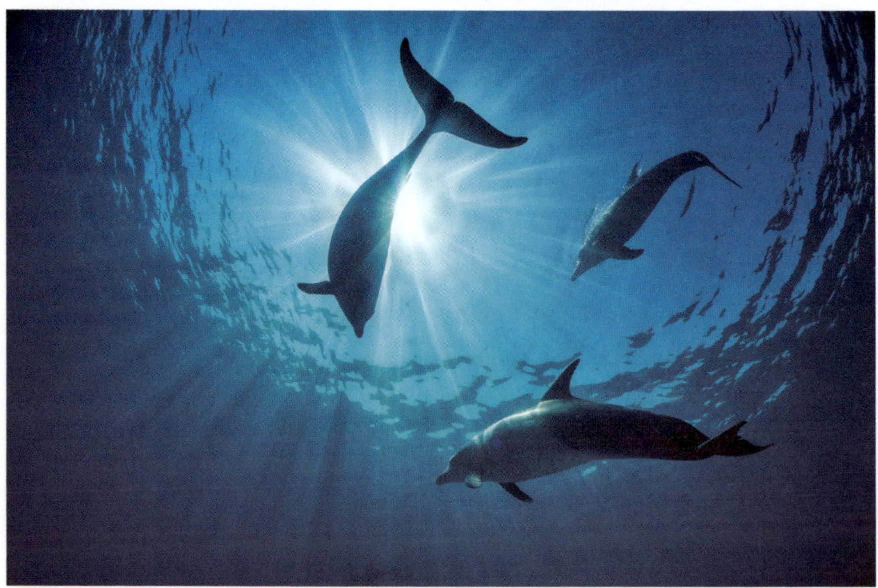

SUMPTUOUS SUNBURSTS

Whenever I show an attractive sunburst shot to a group of photographers, someone invariably asks me what settings I used. Settings, of course, matter, but there is a myth in underwater photography that there are some mystical settings that transform the unattractive blob of the sun into a beautiful sunburst. There aren't—the key ingredients happen outside the camera. When the water is sheltered from the wind, the smooth surface will focus sunlight into attractive beams, and if you stay reasonably shallow you will avoid a cyan halo around the sun, giving you everything you need to fill your images with sumptuous sunbursts.

This assignment is designed to help you develop a clear sense of how surface conditions, your depth, and the height of the sun control the photographic potential of a sunburst. Building this knowledge lets you plan sunburst images pre-dive and to decide when you'll be keeping the sun well out of shot, and to capture it in all its glory when the conditions are optimum.

An ideal time to do this assignment is when you drop in and are greeted by beautiful beams. Take a series of available-light shots every 3ft (1m) you descend. Review the shots in-camera and make a call about what depth range gives the best images on that dive. Ascend to this depth and start searching for subjects to shoot against the sun. Sticking to the optimal depth range rather than chasing up and down the reef after creatures will make a big difference to your sunburst images.

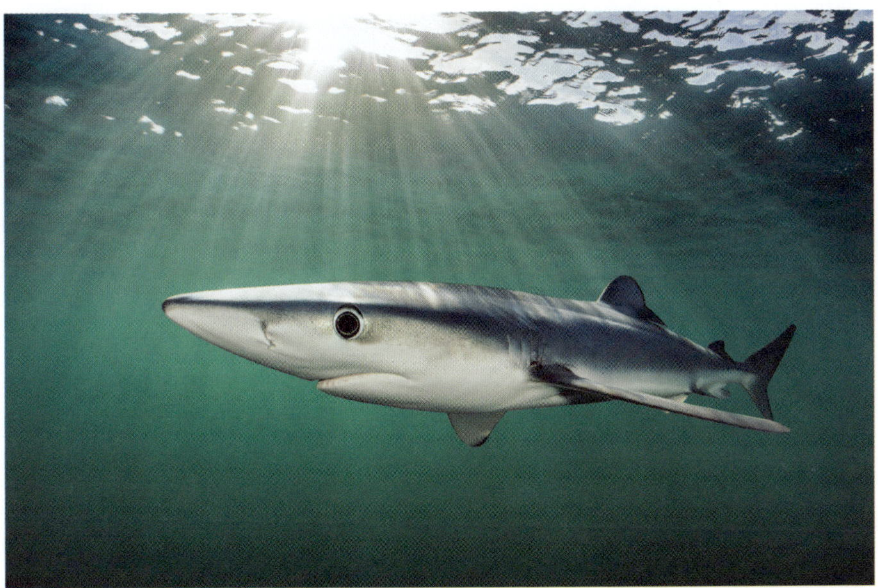

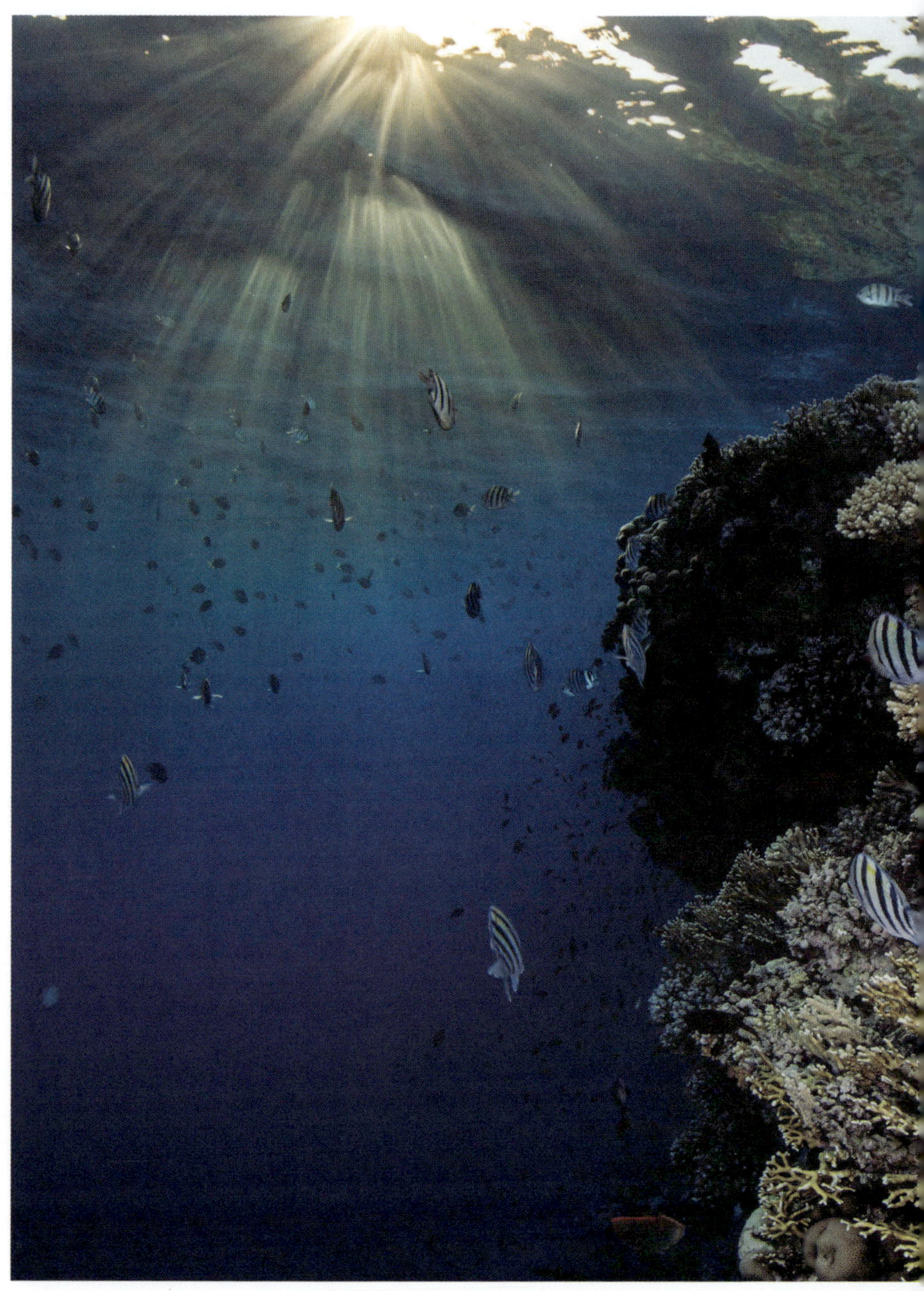

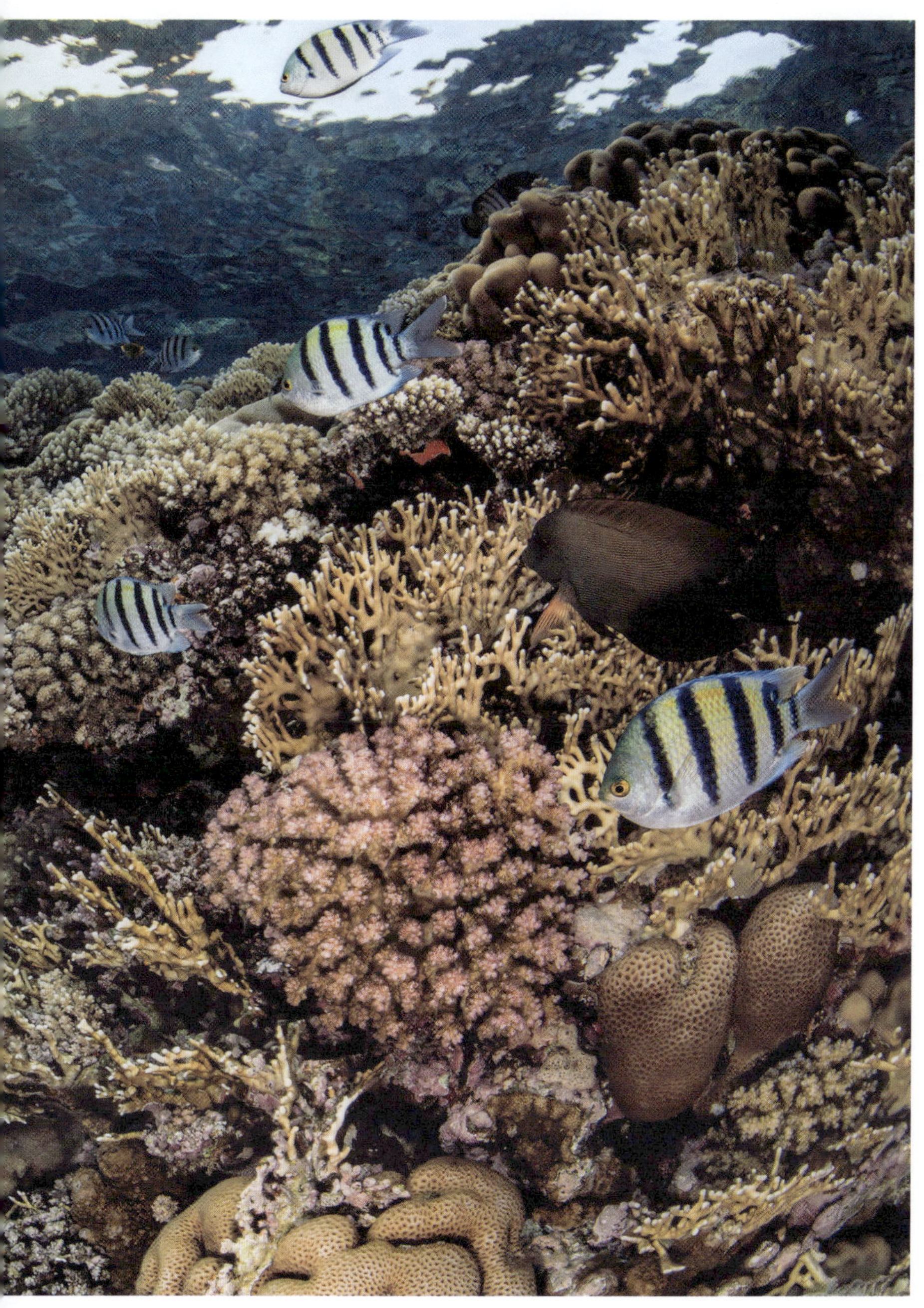

▲ *The conditions and the depth you dive to are the most important factors for shooting sunbursts. When the sun is low, you need to stay very close to the surface for beautiful light.*

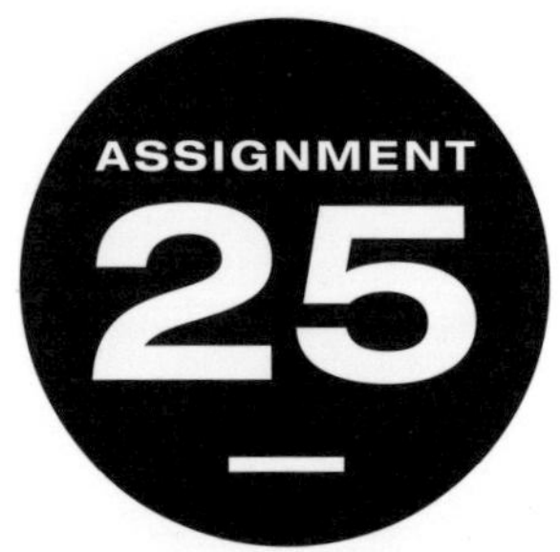

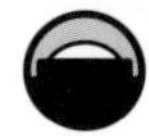
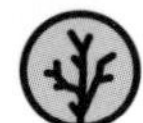
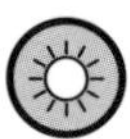

TIPS

- Flash drains the atmosphere out of cavern images, so shoot with available light unless there is an exceptional subject that demands to be illuminated.

- Use back-button focus, which is a technique that uses different buttons for focusing and operating the shutter. Light beams can confuse autofocus systems, and it is safer to carefully focus once and not have to refocus while shooting a series of images.

▶ *Shoot from the shadow toward the light and hide anything brighter than the beams in your composition. Settings in caverns are always a compromise.*

BEAM ME UP

Caverns are much loved by underwater photographers for their unique blend of subject matter. Many coral reefs have caves cutting into them, which can be packed with colorful soft corals and even schools of glassfish or silversides, while freshwater caverns offer up captivating rock formations such as stalactites. The subject that unites both are shafts of light, whose photographic potential has boomed as each generation of digital cameras has rewritten the rules with advancements in higher ISOs and noise control and in-body image stabilization (IBIS). Your assignment is to capture these beautiful shafts of light.

Caverns are dark and require you to recalibrate what you consider "normal" underwater photography settings, which makes this an excellent brief for expanding your creative horizons. That said, you can't be quite as free with very high ISOs as land photographers because of the monochromatic nature of underwater light. Shooting beams is a balancing act because you ideally want a closed aperture for corner sharpness, a fast shutter speed to freeze the beams, and a low ISO for image quality, but in truth, you will have to compromise on all three. It is easy to have jump settings for diving in a sunny, shallow sea, but it's impossible for caverns because the light varies so much shot to shot.

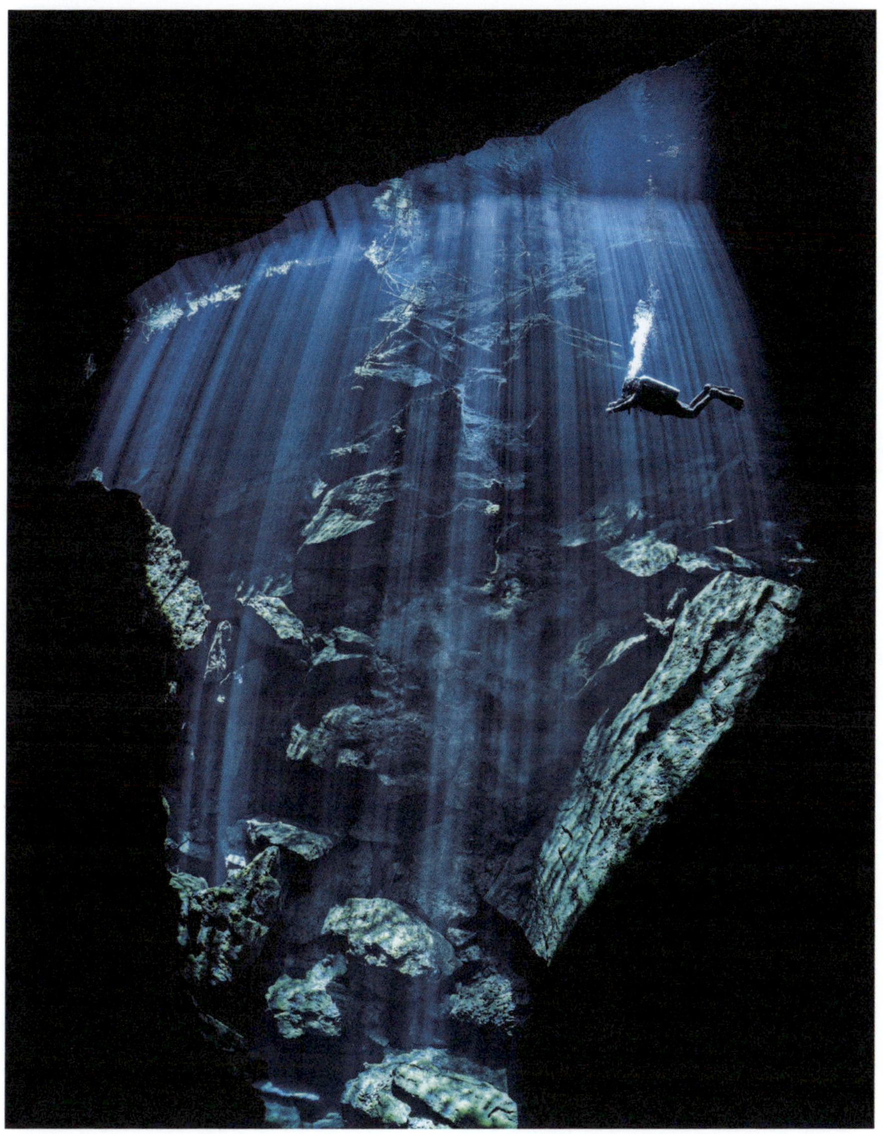

Many caverns only get attractive beams in the middle of the day when the sun is high enough to shine down into the opening. The calmer the water, the more tightly focused the beams will appear. Stay in the dark and shoot toward the light, as the better you can hide the bright surface from the camera, the more easily you can expose for beams. Compositionally, beams look best when they start and finish in the frame. Consider using a non-fisheye wideangle to keep them straight.

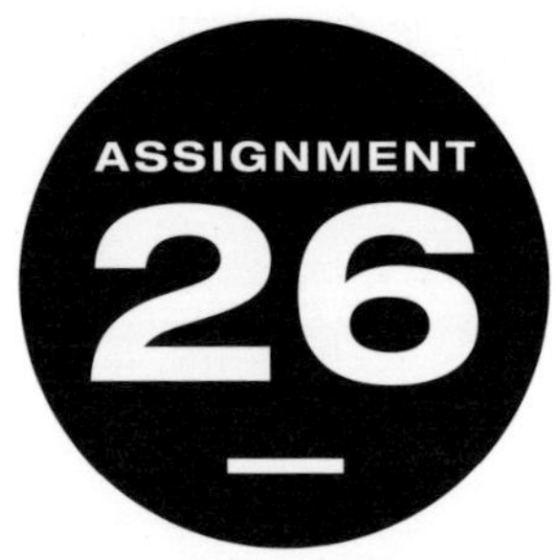

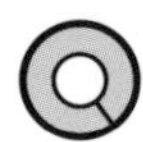
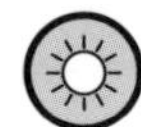

TIPS

- Use a fast shutter speed (such as the camera's shortest flash synchronization speed) and a closed aperture with a snoot to keep the surroundings dark. The lighting gives separation in the image, so there is no need to use a shallow depth of field.

- Snoots are also great for backlighting. Once you've mastered aiming them yourself, this is easy to set up with longer strobe arms.

- Use the snoot's inserts to change the size of the spotlight. It will take a few dives to master before it becomes a straightforward and valuable ability.

IN THE SPOTLIGHT

A snoot restricts the light from a flash into a narrow beam that is typically used to illuminate a subject but not its surroundings. They can be simple tubes fitted to the front of a strobe, but these days most designs include a lens to make the most of your flash power and create a focused spotlight. Snoot photography is highly suited to muck diving, letting you reveal the fantastic beasts you discover without lighting up the muddy sand they are living on.

Fortunately, most muck dives are made with expert guides, who are usually experienced photo assistants and know exactly how to aim a snoot. You should always make the most of any opportunity to work with a guide (see Assignment 30). However, your brief here is to shoot snoot-lit pictures without any help. This is a valuable skill because it means your snoot lighting is not confined to the destinations with dedicated guides. Also, once you have the knack for aiming a snoot yourself, you will be surprised how easy it is.

Position the snoot above the port, aligned parallel to the lens and angled down toward the subject. Start by framing the subject and focus on it with back-button focus. Now, using the aiming light of the strobe, angle the snoot so that it lights the subject. Take a photo and see how the light looks. If the light is too low in the frame, move closer, refocus, and reshoot. If the light is too high, back away slightly and do the same. So long as you don't refocus, you now know that any subject that comes into focus will also be in the light when the strobe fires.

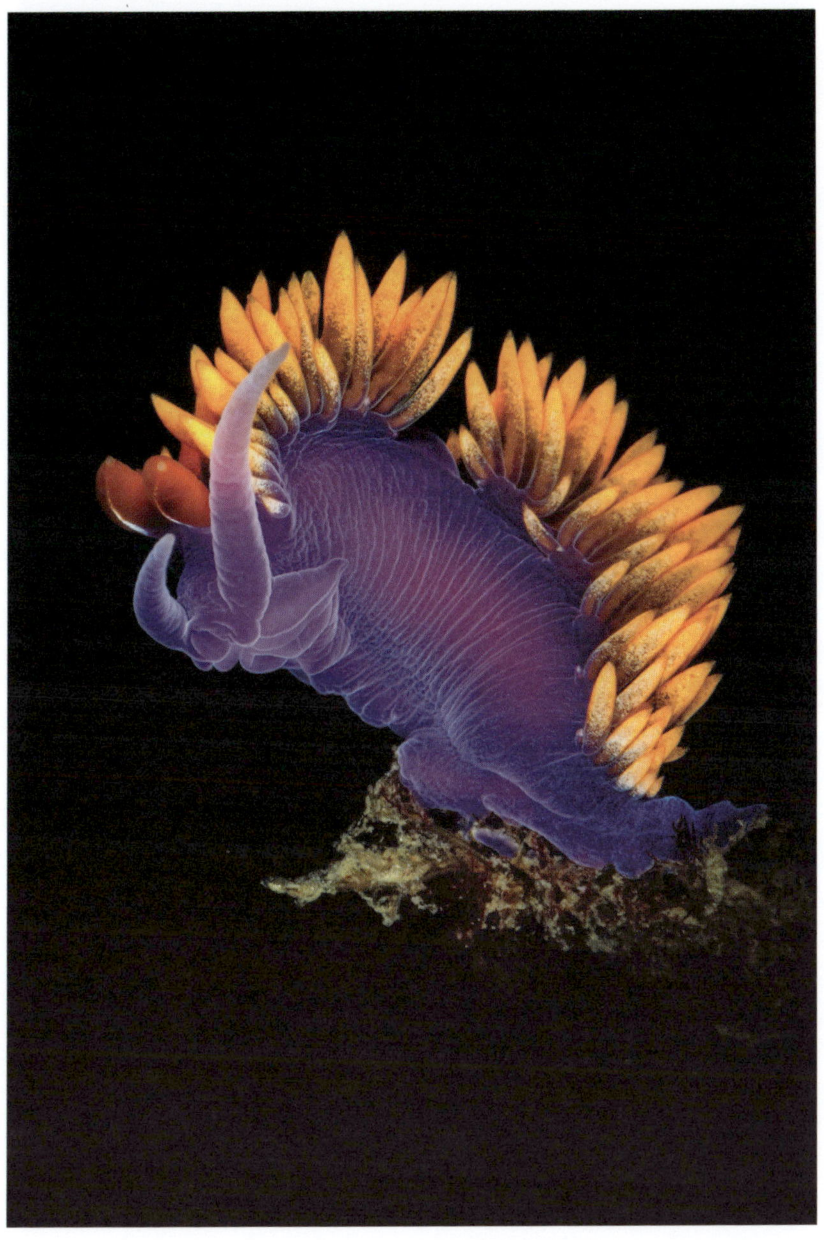

▲ Diving on the coast of California,
there aren't dedicated dive guides, but
there are beautiful nudibranchs ideal for
snoot photography.

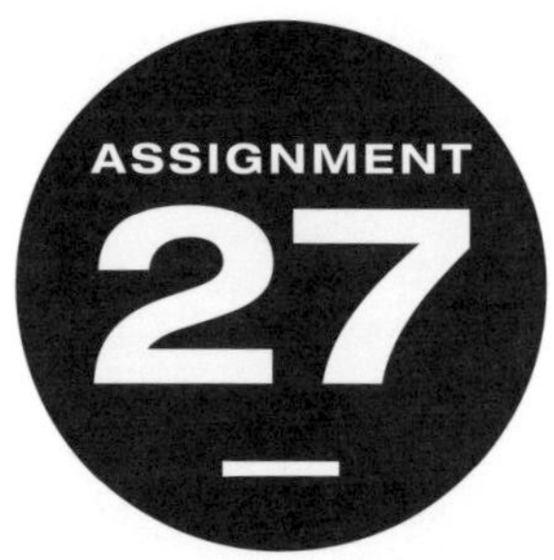

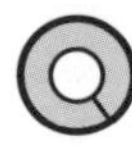

▶ *Intentional camera movement combined with snoot lighting reveals a sharp goby and attractive textures in the sea pen.*

SNOOT WITH MOVEMENT

Classic snoot shots of a creature in the spotlight are highly impactful, but over time they become repetitive. Fortunately, as you develop your snoot-aiming skills, you open up other creative options. For this assignment, I want you to combine snoot lighting with long exposures that liven up the negative space in the image (negative space simply refers to the parts of the picture that are not the subject). A pure black background is a perfectly acceptable type of negative space, but here you should be aiming for something more creative.

This technique becomes particularly interesting when intentional camera movement (ICM), typically panning, is used during the long exposure. The snooted strobe light freezes the subject, while the ICM creates attractive textures from the surroundings. Generating this type of blur requires a shutter speed between 1/15 sec. and 1/4 sec., which is a long enough exposure to create blur, yet short enough to be controllable. You still need to balance the other camera settings, so set a low ISO and small aperture to ensure the blue is properly exposed.

I always use front-curtain flash sync, so that the flash fires at the start of the exposure. This ensures that the main subject is perfectly in focus and frozen exactly where intended in the composition before I start the ICM technique. Thinking of the image as a two-stage process definitely helps in producing these shots.

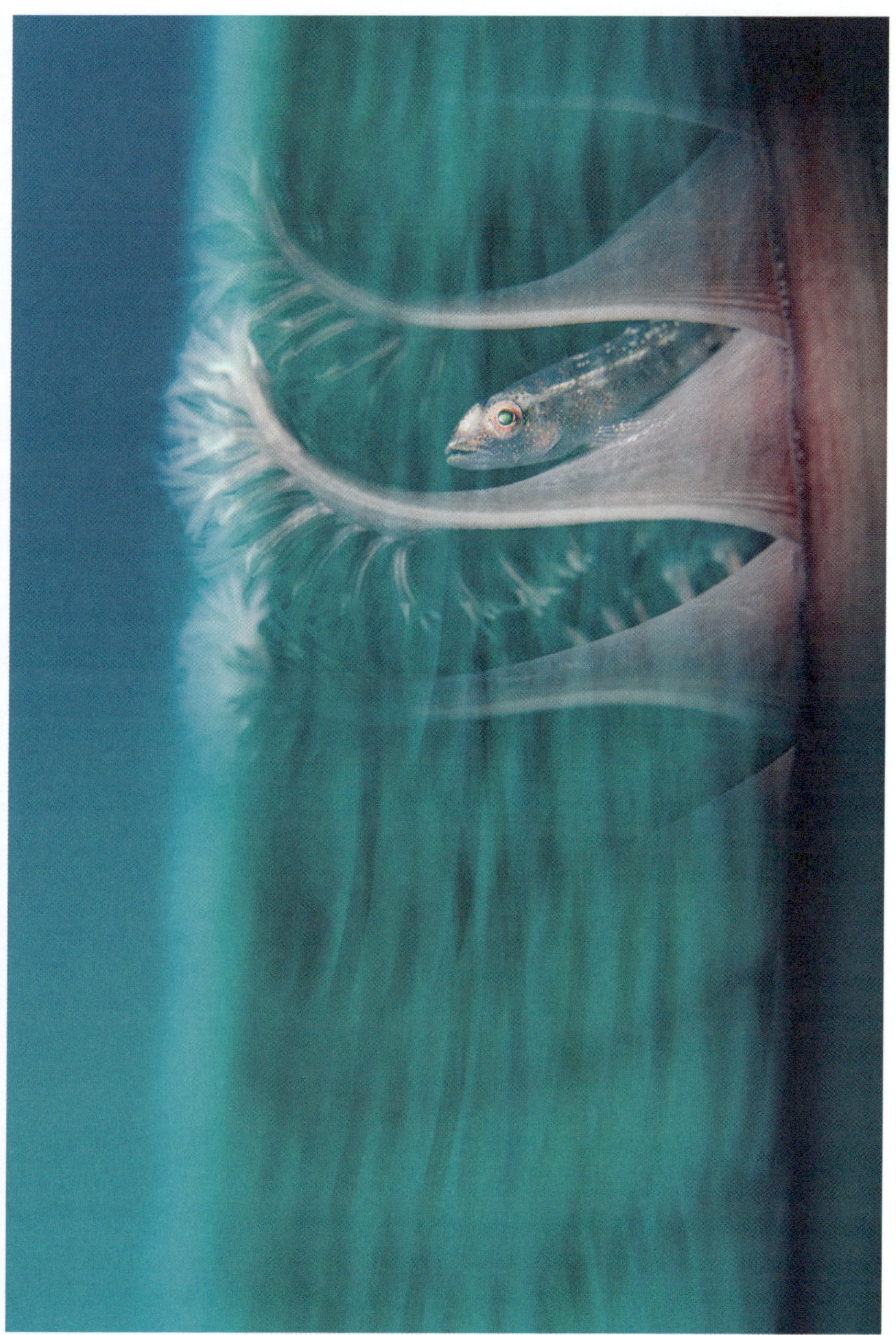

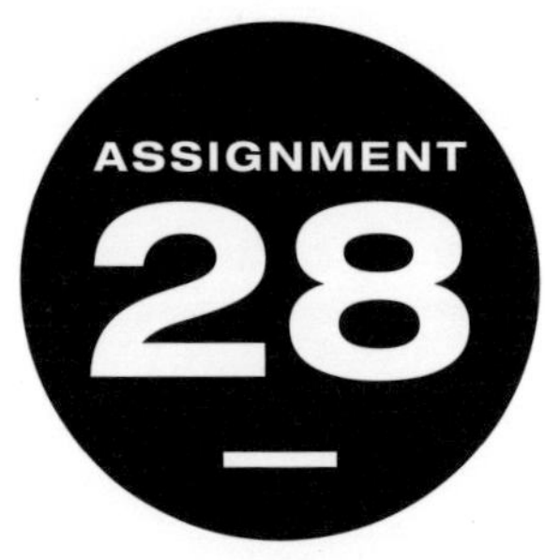

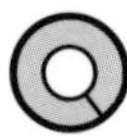

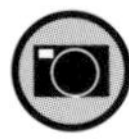

TIPS

- There is no magical aperture setting for achieving the optimum depth of field in macro shooting. Instead, the best approach is to shoot, review, and adjust until you achieve the desired effect, remembering the shortcut technique from Assignment 12.

- Don't get fixated on the subject when framing and reviewing your shots. Remember to consider the negative space and adjust your composition, lighting, and settings to optimize the entire frame for a standout shot.

SIMPLE IS STRONG

Antoine de Saint-Exupéry, the author of *The Little Prince*, famously said, "Perfection is achieved, not when there is nothing more to add, but when there is nothing left to take away." His words are an excellent guiding principle for macro photography, especially underwater, which is regularly characterized by a real riot of life. The challenge of simplifying your compositions is the theme of this macro assignment. Shoot and then carefully review each photo, asking yourself if every element is contributing. If it isn't, get rid of it. Simple images are always eye-catching—and very popular on social media.

In macro photography, there are a host of techniques for simplifying images. Perhaps the easiest is framing a subject against open water, creating a clean black background. A similar effect can be achieved with a snoot, as we discussed in Assignments 26 and 27. For this assignment, however, the simplifying technique is to use a shallow depth of field to blur any distractions. In macro shooting, this can be achieved by opening the aperture or moving closer, if only by a small amount—macro photographers often overlook how powerfully depth of field can be reduced by increasing subject magnification.

Also consider how the position of the subject in its environment impacts its photographic potential. It is common to encounter several individuals of a species on a dive, but one may offer far more potential than the others because where it lives will have an impact on how the rest of the frame will photograph.

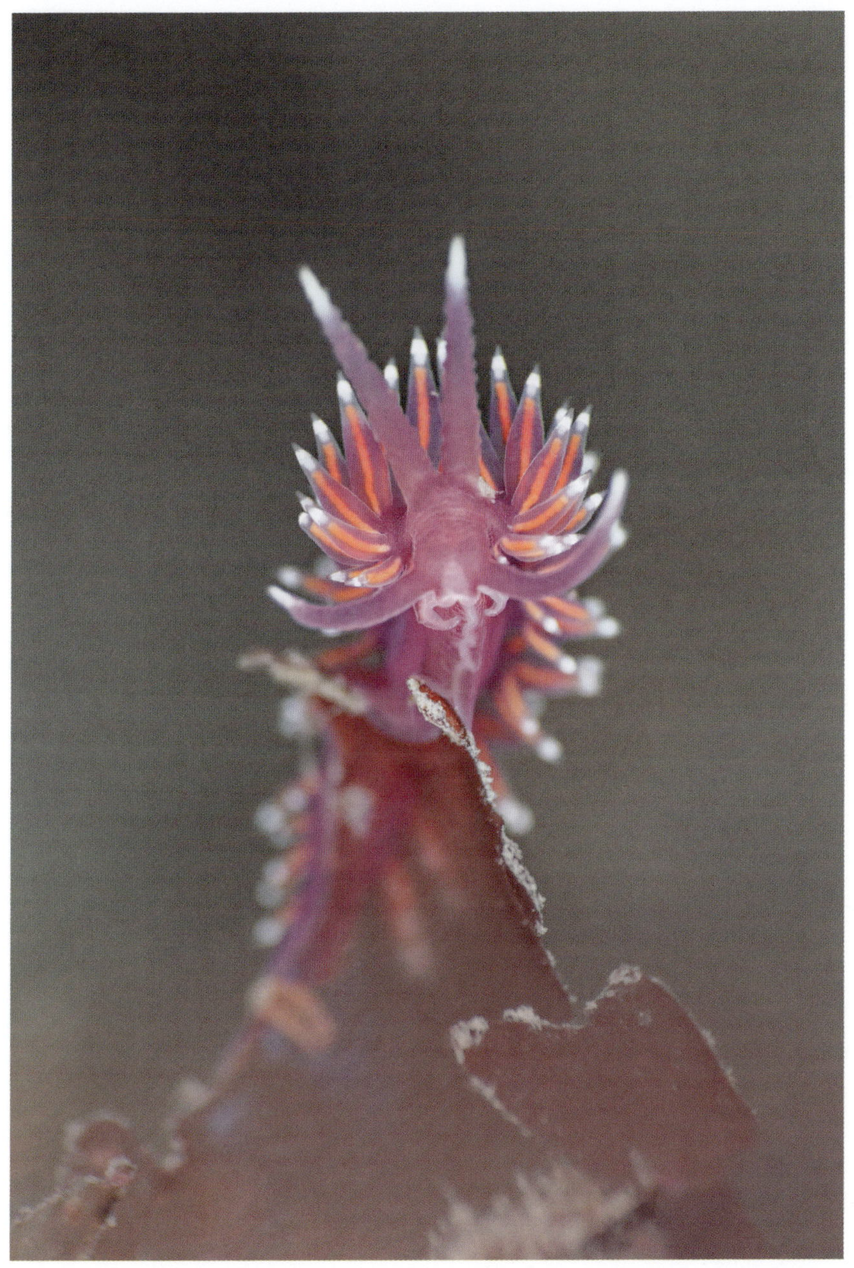

▲ This slug was in the shallows on a poor-
visibility day in the UK, but by eliminating
distractions, I created a memorable shot.

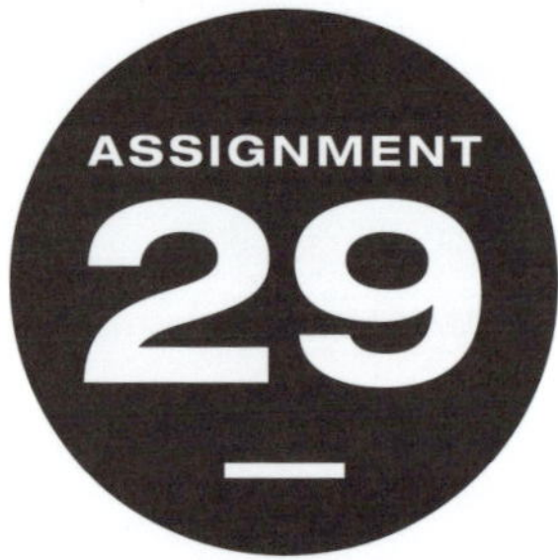

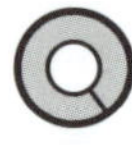

TIPS

- Start with lower-powered supermacro accessories and build up to higher-magnification work. In stores, everyone is seduced by wanting the most powerful lenses, but underwater the less powerful lenses are much easier to use and suit more subjects.

- Supermacro is easiest when everything is stable, so start using this technique in benign diving conditions and with stationary subjects.

▼ *Supermacro photography introduces you to amazing creatures. Shaun the Sheep slugs are the size of the tip of a pencil.*

▶ *Being able to hold your camera perfectly still is critical when so close to tiny animals, like these pygmy gobies.*

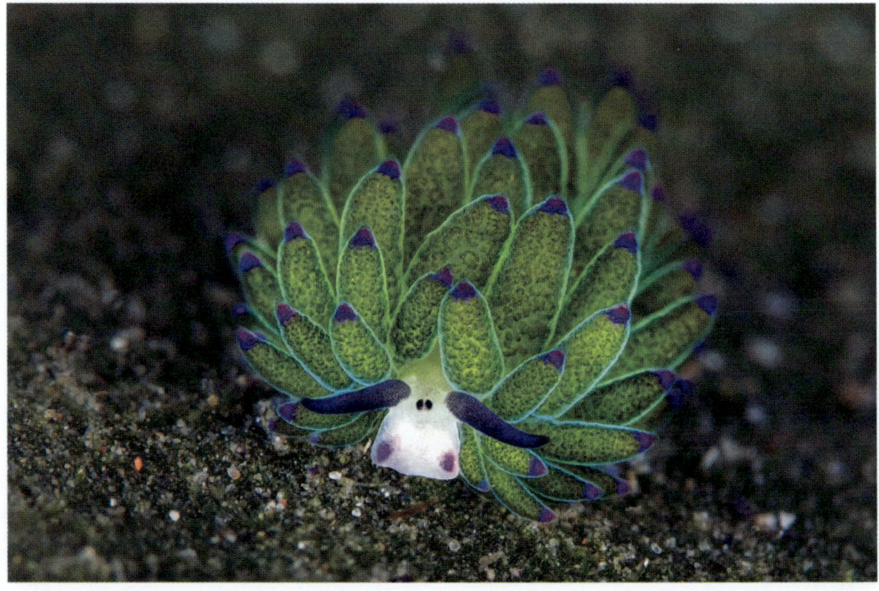

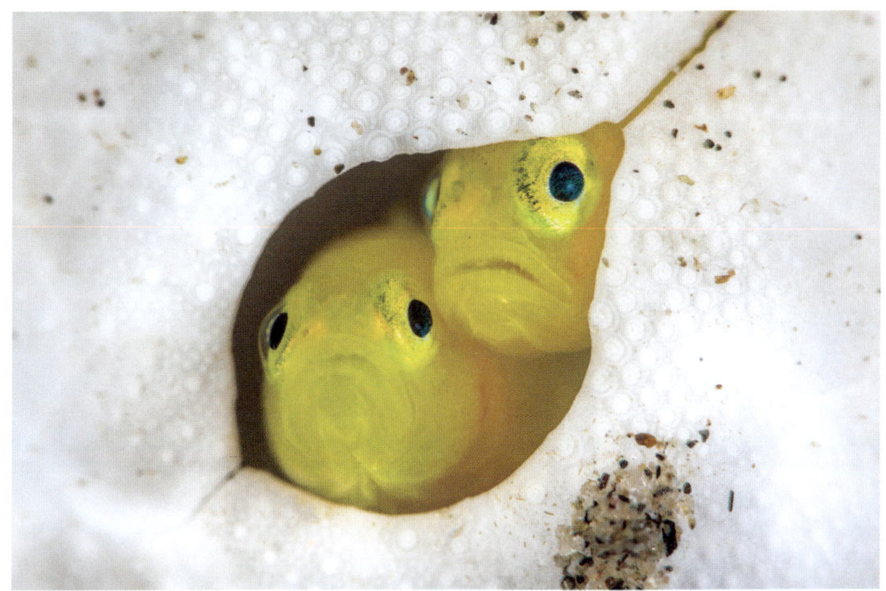

GO SUPER

Why be normal when you can be super? The aim of this assignment is to produce tack-sharp pictures of the tiniest macro subjects by going beyond 1:1 magnification and into the realm of supermacro. This is a fascinating branch of underwater photography, not just for the otherworldly animals it depicts, but also because the imagery can be truly stunning, as the razor-thin depth of field blurs everything beyond the subject, making your images pop.

Supermacro shooting is challenging in practice because of the difficulty of accurately finding, focusing, and framing the subject. Arguably the biggest challenge is finding your subjects through the viewfinder. This is difficult because you don't just need to aim left-right, up-down, but also need to be exactly the right distance away for the subject to be in focus enough to see. When shooting tiny critters, I always line up my lens by looking over the top of the camera first, making sure the end of the lens is pointing at the subject and, from experience, the right distance away for the supermacro accessory I'm using. Only then do I go to the viewfinder.

Most supermacro photographers find that focusing is easiest when the AF-ON button is used (which most underwater housings provide access to with a lever that falls under your left thumb). This means you can use the AF to get the focus approximately correct, then stop using AF and fine-tune both the focus and composition by moving the camera very slightly.

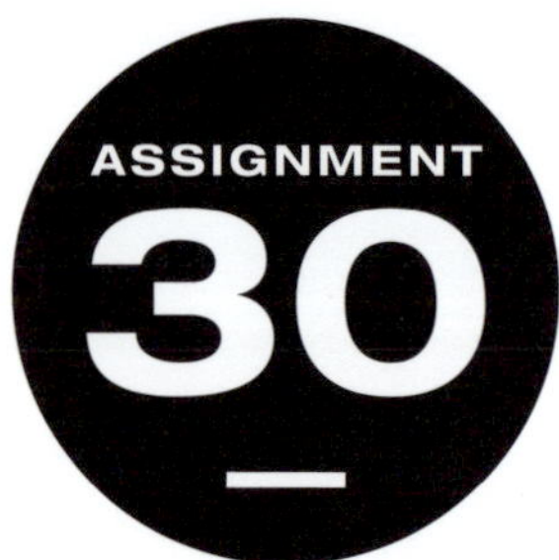

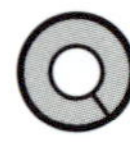

TIPS

- The less looking after you need, the more time your guide has to find the best subjects. Dive well and pay attention to instructions and dives will be much more productive.

- Most guides care deeply about the species we photograph, but unethical nature photographers can encourage them to push the limits by harassing subjects. Don't be this photographer.

▼ *Guides will show you creatures you'd never be able to find yourself.*

▶ *Guides can also help with advanced lighting techniques.*

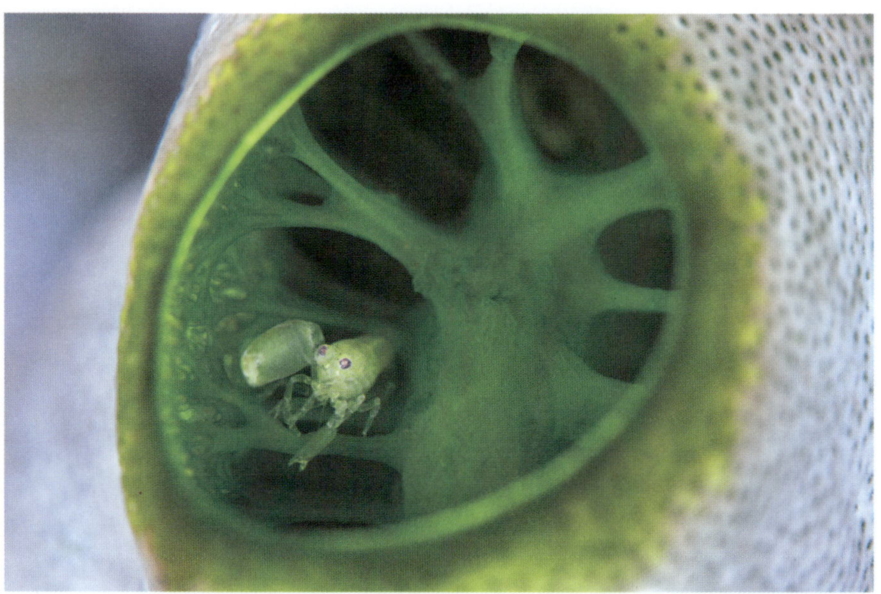

WORK WITH A GUIDE

In many of the most popular macro photography destinations, diving is done in small groups with specialist guides. These naturalist guides are highly experienced in the local marine life and are eagle-eyed spotters. They can also be very helpful photography assistants, holding lighting accessories such as snoots or positioning items that can be used as artificial backgrounds. To maximize the photographic potential of such macro trips, it is essential to work seamlessly with a guide.

This assignment should run throughout your next trip to one such macro destination, with the goal of producing a quality portfolio of macro shots. Challenge yourself to communicate with your guide, tell them about the species you are interested in, and use your phone and social media to show them the types of shots you are chasing. Guides try and please all their guests, but this usually means showing everyone the same star creatures. Communication encourages the guides to treat you differently, ensuring you don't go home with just the same shots as everyone else.

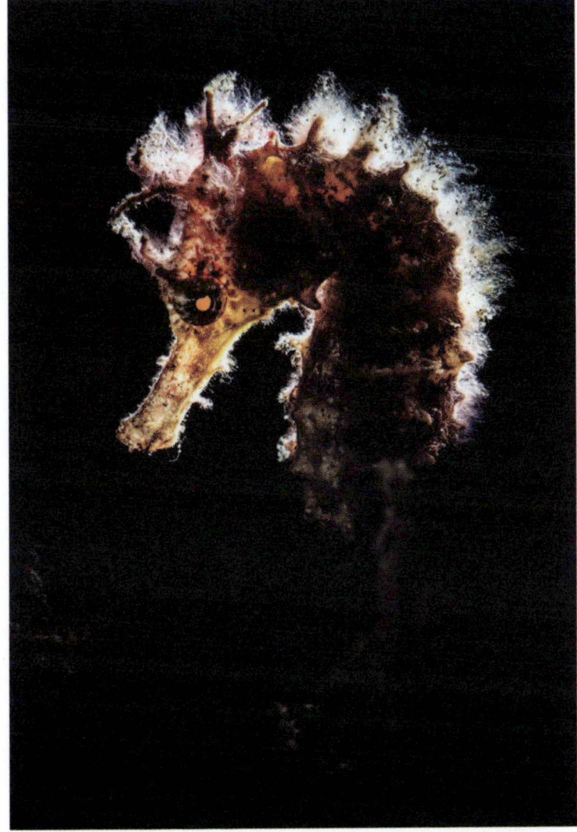

When working with a guide, always aim for some images you couldn't easily produce alone. If you have a spare flash or bright flashlight, consider asking them to hold this to light your subjects from unusual angles, or to hold a background (black or white dive slate or sparkly, reflective material) behind the subject. Once you have selected your best shots from each day, spend time at the dive center showing them to your guide, making sure to praise their contribution. Listen to their ideas and generate your own ideas of how you can improve the following day.

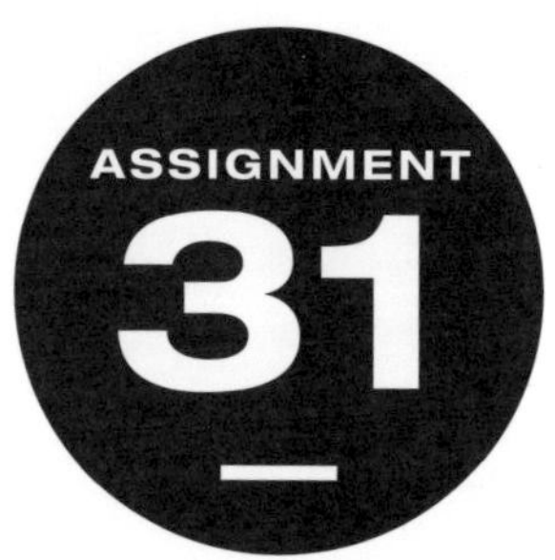

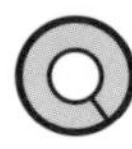

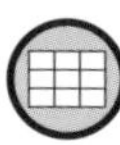

TIPS

- Small-in-the-frame shots can be too subtle to win you likes on social media, but they usually score big in contests, magazines, and as prints.

- Choose your widest macro lens for these shots, so that you can still shoot close while including more space around the subject.

- Shoot the scene at a range of magnifications and evaluate which composition works best once you've downloaded the shots.

▶ *Symbiotic creatures are ideal for small-in-the-frame compositions. Avoid central compositions to emphasize the diminutive proportions of the subject.*

SMALL IN THE FRAME

The aim of macro photography is to reveal the tiny wonders of the ocean, and the aim of this assignment is to amaze people with photos that truly show how small they are. As beginners, we're taught to get close and fill the frame, but this assignment encourages you to change your approach while understanding the limits.

When we fill the frame with a subject, the picture is invariably packed with content. So, the main challenge of composing with macro subjects small in the frame is making the whole image worth looking at. This makes subject selection critical. Seek out symbiotic animals, such as an anemonefish in an anemone, a pygmy seahorse on a sea fan, or a shrimp living on the patterned body of a sea cucumber. Let the natural patterns in the host creature define your composition and compose with the subject facing into the frame. If you position a small subject in the center of the frame, this suggests that you couldn't get close enough. However, compose it off-center and you invite the viewer to explore the frame. Keep the camera reasonably parallel to the scene and close the aperture to maximize the depth of field.

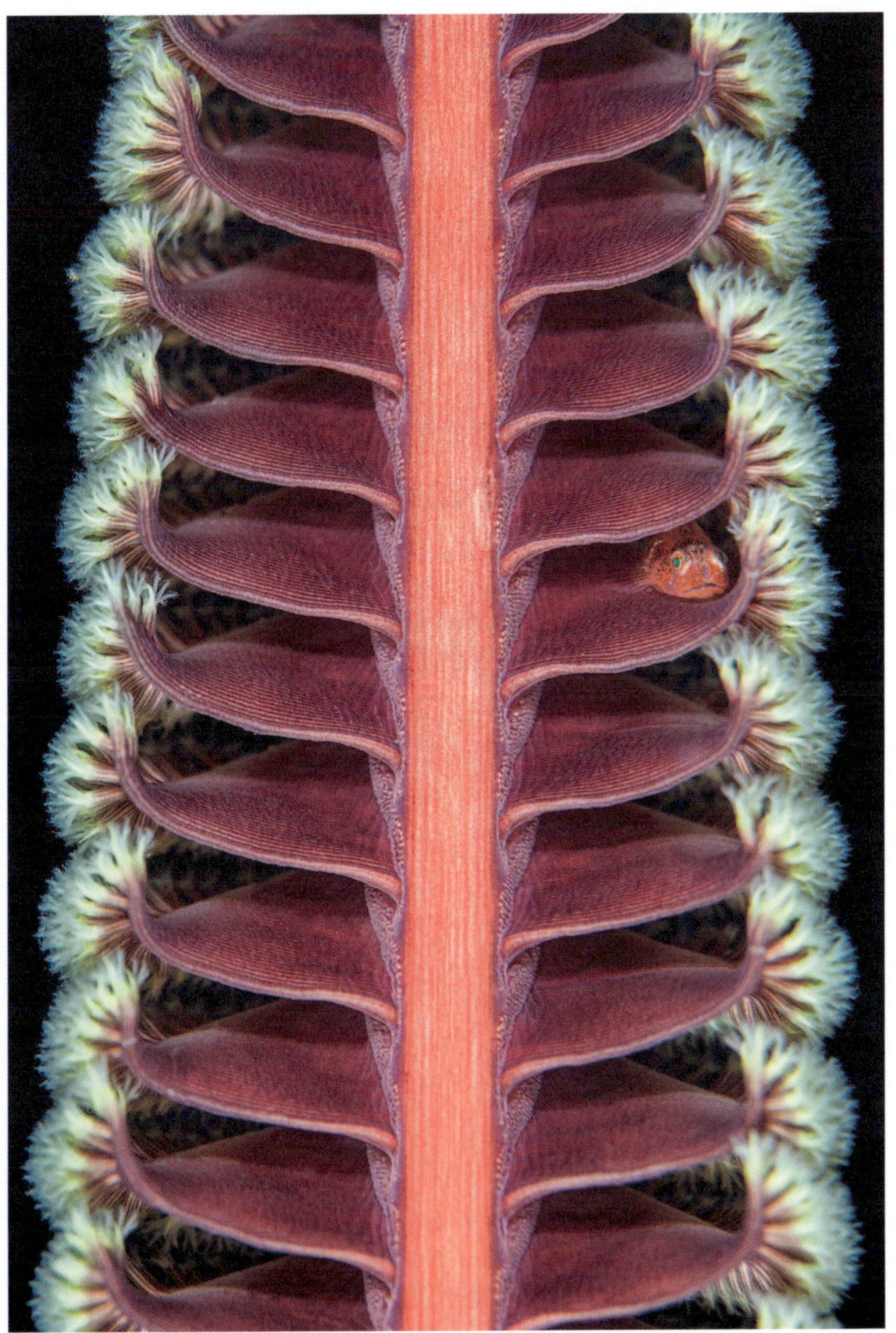

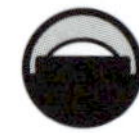
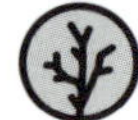
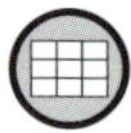

TIPS

- A fisheye zoom lens, such as Nauticam's FCP, is ideal for this assignment because you can use the zoom to shrink and enlarge the background, letting you frame a wider range of foregrounds against it.

- When shooting upward toward a background with a wideangle lens, your own breath in the form of bubbles will trail through your picture. Once you've optimized settings, swim away, breathe out, then return without breathing out again to shoot the picture.

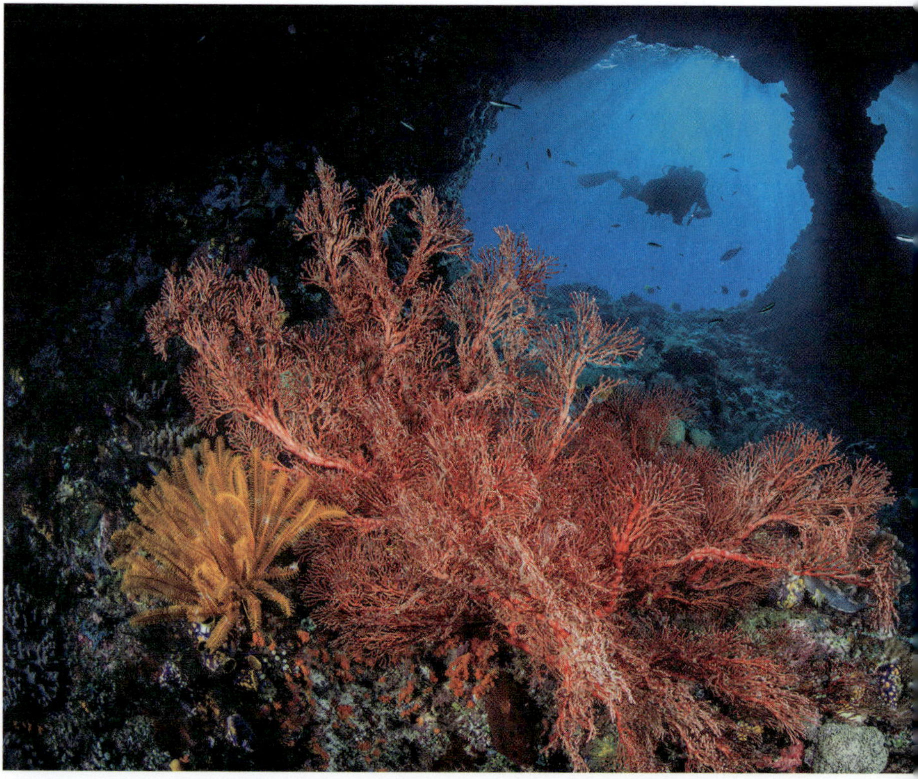

WORK THE BACKGROUND

There are many dive sites around the world that are famed for scenic wideangle underwater photography. Examples range from Salt Pier in Bonaire to Boo Windows in Raja Ampat. The reason that these sites are productive is not because they have more colorful sponges and corals than other places, but because of the attractive backgrounds they offer. The underwater world is packed with amazing foregrounds for wideangle photography, but attractive backgrounds that complete these compositions are much harder to find.

Finding, exploiting, and appreciating wideangle backgrounds is the focus of this assignment. If you are on a reef or wall, drop down a little so you have at least 15ft (5m) of topography above you to create a backdrop. Look for an interesting outcrop or overhang that will make a pleasing background. It will photograph even better if it has some architecturally interesting sea fans or table corals growing out of it, all of which add to the visual interest. Another go-to are layers of reef at different distances, which create an even stronger sense of depth in the composition.

A fun part of this assignment is to see how many different foreground subjects you can shoot against a single background. Note how the atmosphere of the shot changes as you move around the background and the angle of the ambient light changes. Choose two shots of different foregrounds and show them to your dive buddies, who are unlikely to notice they were taken in the same place. This assignment demonstrates the value of a quality background and reminds you that finding one is the priority when shooting wideangle scenery.

◄ *Reefs with interesting topography are particularly good for wideangle shots. A single feature can usually be framed with a handful of different foregrounds.*

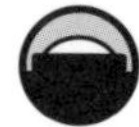

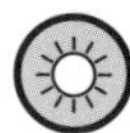
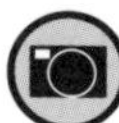

TIPS

- Always use your best flashgun as an off-camera strobe, and use an older flashgun as the on-camera trigger.

- Use your remote flash's aiming light to give you an idea of where the light will be falling.

OFF-CAMERA STROBE

Off-camera strobes are a powerful and creative advanced technique but take a few dives to master. Save this assignment for a reasonably shallow wreck dive where you can safely get into darker areas and spend time experimenting with different shots, both with the off-camera light going away from the camera, and with it coming toward the lens. You should aim to produce one good shot with each style of lighting over the course of a few dives.

An easy way to start is using a powerful video light because they are easier to aim—the light you see is the light you get. These will teach you where to place lights but will be frustrating because they lack power and control in most conditions, and you will soon want to switch to strobes. Although strobes have built-in optical triggers, it is much better to use a dedicated slave trigger on a short cable. This allows you to position the flash trigger in view of the camera but hide the flash out of sight. In compelling off-camera strobe shots, the light seems to magically appear, because the source remains hidden. Attach a GorillaPod to the remote strobe to be able to accurately aim and position it—and fit a clip so you can carry it.

If you want the off-camera strobe to be the only visible light source in the photo, set it to full power and use just one normal on-camera flash set to low power to trigger it. Alternatively, slow down the exposure to allow ambient light into the image, and add normal front strobe lighting when required.

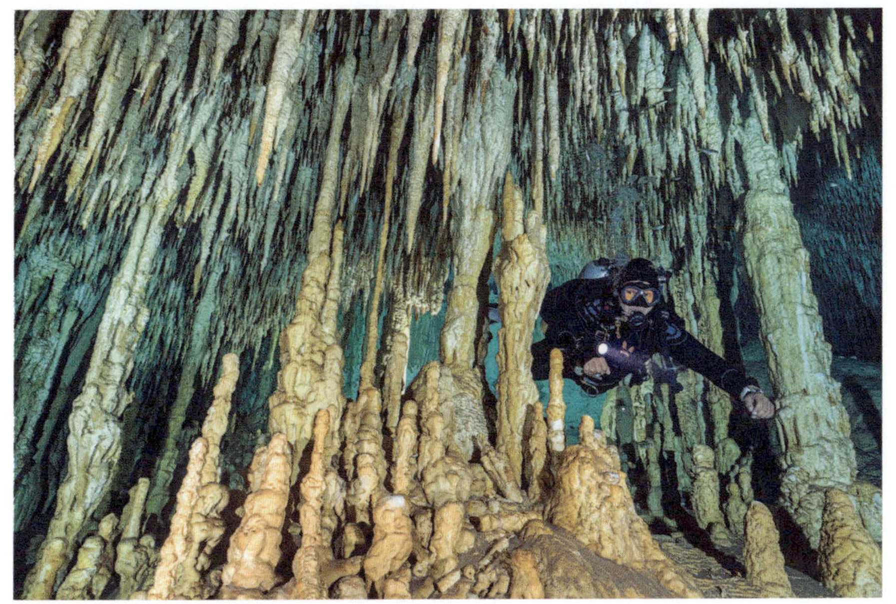

▲ *Off-camera flash can be used subtly—this image would be dominated by black without the third strobe lighting the background.*

▼ *Backlighting with off-camera strobes creates a dramatic image—there is a strobe behind each motorbike wheel.*

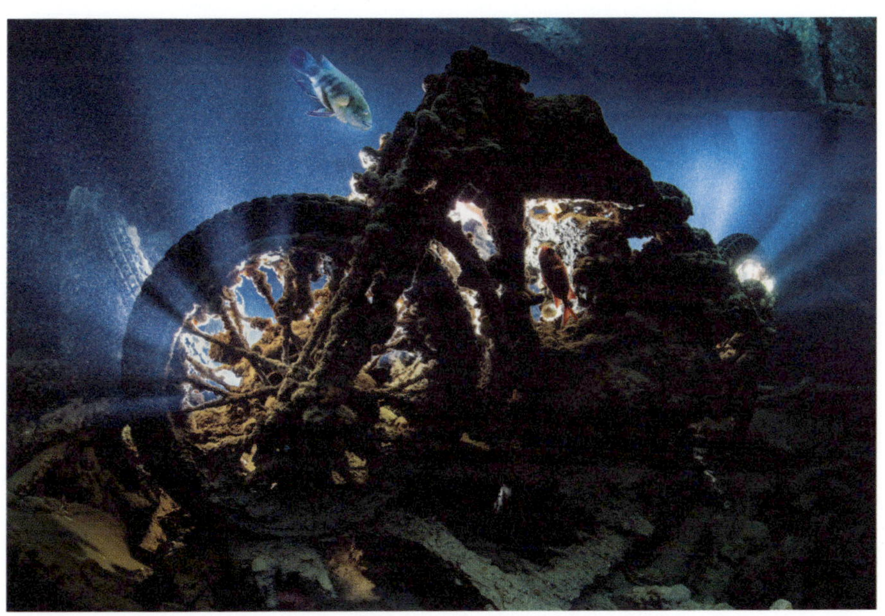

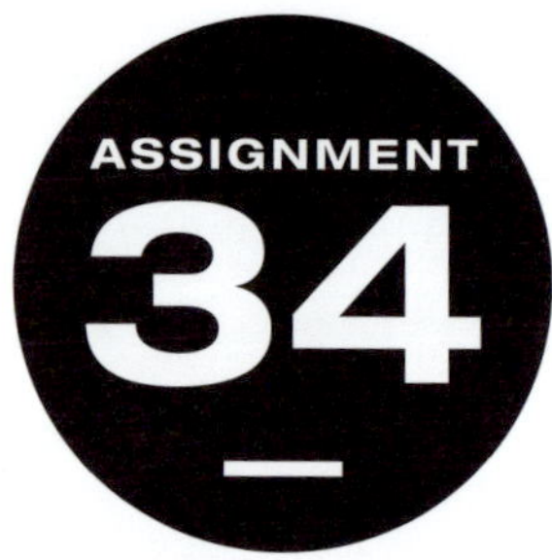

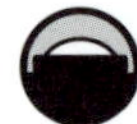

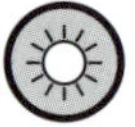

TIPS

- You can produce colorful wreck images by just using white balance or just using filters, but it is the combination of the two that produces the best results. Remember, the better the starting point, the better the finished picture, no matter how good the processing tools.

- Sunlight is your light source, so it is critical to use it well. Pay attention to the direction and work with it.

- Manually setting the camera's white balance on the wreck will give great colors straight out of the camera. If it doesn't work, don't worry—shoot good compositions and fix the white balance in Lightroom.

▼ *Avoid descending all the way to the seabed. Instead, shoot from wreck level or even slightly shallower.*

▶ *Don't overcompensate when adjusting the white balance. Instead, aim to keep the water a rich color.*

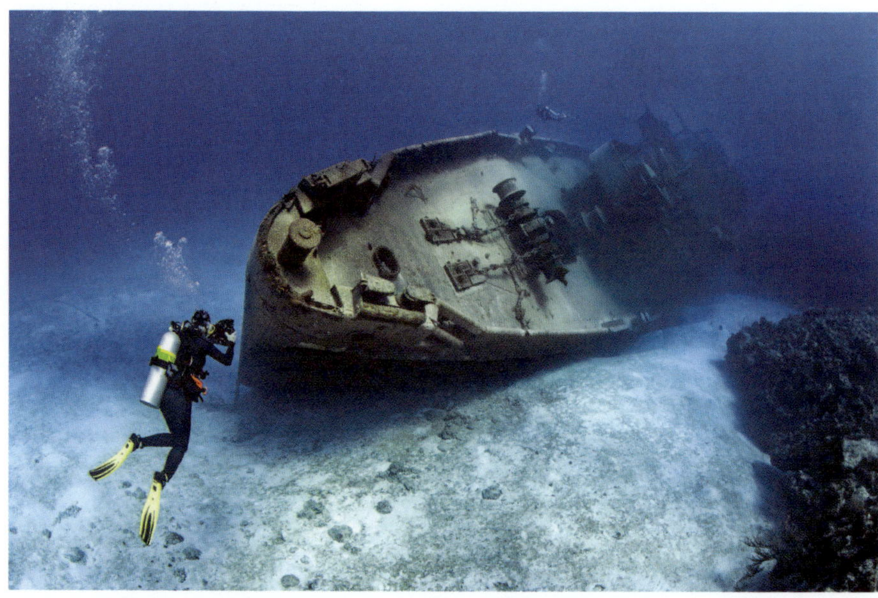

FULL-COLOR WRECK

The most spectacular shipwreck images are those showing a whole wreck resting on the bottom of the sea. Such scenes require our widest fisheye lenses but will invariably be far too big to light effectively with flash. In fact, your flashes will only light up backscatter, so their optimum setting is off. However, a lack of flash doesn't have to mean a lack of color, and for many photographers the most stunning wreck images are ones taken in available light, where a combination of white balance and underwater correction filters produce realistic color from the wreck and maintain a rich blue in the background water.

This assignment uses a technique you may not have tried before, so it will not only yield stunning images, but will also help you grow as an underwater photographer. I want you to take a colorful wreck image without flash. You will need a reasonably shallow wreck—one in less than 65ft (20m) of water—and you will want to time your dive for sunny conditions, when the sun is striking the wreck's most attractive features.

Wrecks don't move, but the position of the sun does, so timing is everything. Research wrecks you plan to dive to learn their photographic prime times. Shooting in the same direction as the ambient light will always give the best color and detail. Avoid the temptation to sink straight to the seabed—the light comes from above the wreck, so hover in mid-water at the level of the wreck and shoot slightly downward toward the features of interest.

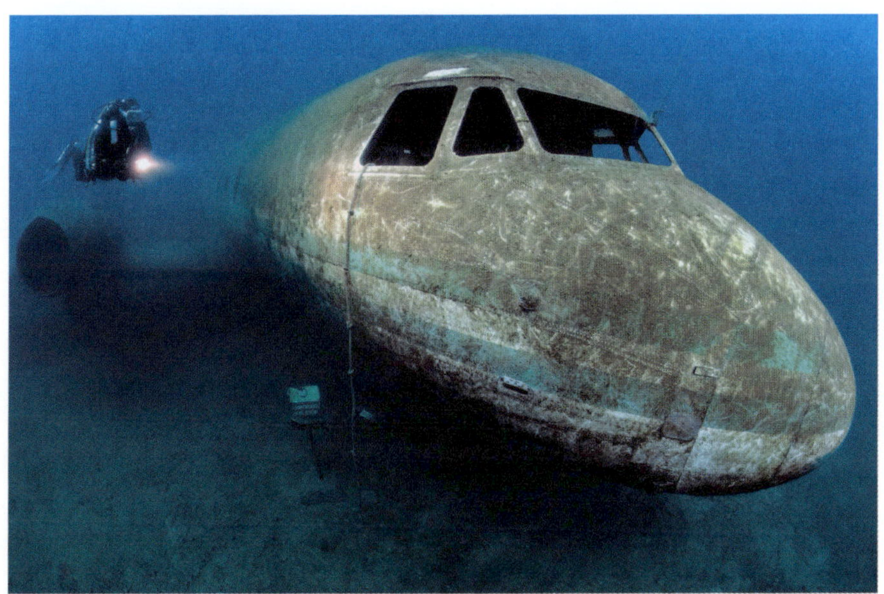

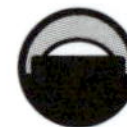
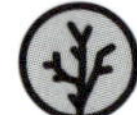

- When it comes to posing, longer fins, reasonably straight legs, and neat arms make for the most attractive silhouettes.

- Most divers look more elegant swimming rather than hovering. Direct your model to swim slowly through the picture, rather than stay still in one spot.

POSE A MODEL

After photographing marine life, divers should, on paper, be an easier subject because they willingly pose for the camera. In reality, this assignment is one of the most challenging because it requires your core photography skills to be on point while introducing plenty of new ones. Model shots rely on communication and cooperation, with two people needing to get everything right at the same time. These photos are harder to produce, but more satisfying when you succeed, especially as two people can be proud of the result.

Your assignment is to produce a series of wideangle images with a well-posed diver silhouette in the background. The process will begin long before you get wet, as you rehearse shots and talk through ideas with your diving buddy. Let them look through your ultra-wideangle lens, so they understand that they don't need to be far away to appear small in the picture. Then discuss how they should pose and suggest swimming across the picture so that their whole silhouette is visible. If they swim directly at the lens, they will just be a small, black blob! Also, remind the model that you need them to pose both clear of the subject and against open water, so they stand out in the shot.

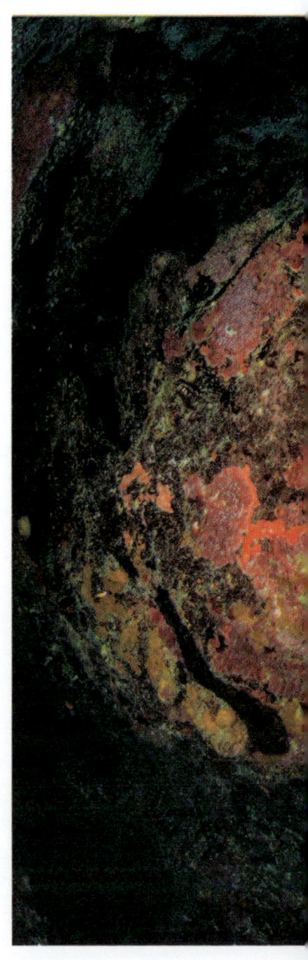

Once underwater, decide on your scene and optimize the shot before calling in the model to pose. This means that you are totally ready to capture the perfect moment and don't waste their energy and enthusiasm while getting your part of the pictures right. Their pose is critical—viewers will be very sensitive to body language, so ensure they are engaged in the scene.

Patience is the other virtue. Posing underwater is difficult, often harder than photographing, and you must always be highly appreciative of anyone willing to give up their dive time for your pictures. Finally, enjoy the process of reviewing and critiquing the images with your buddy, so you are ready to make even better shots.

▼ *Position the model against the blue so they stand out without being obscured by the foreground or blending with the background.*

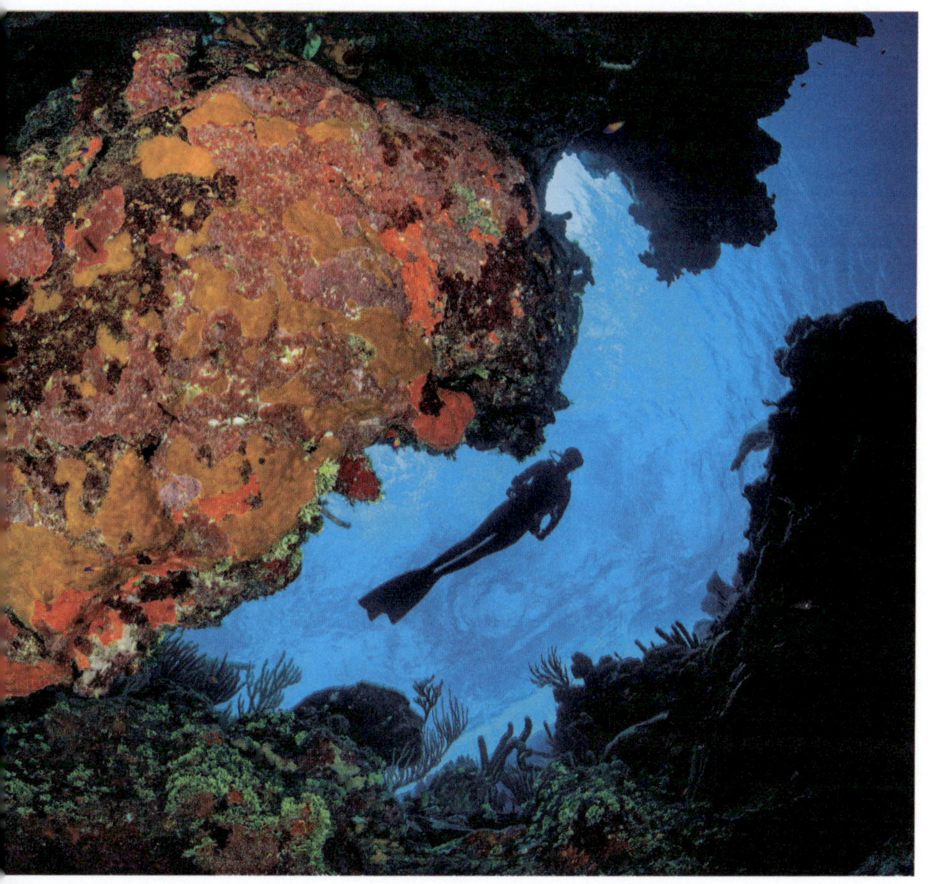

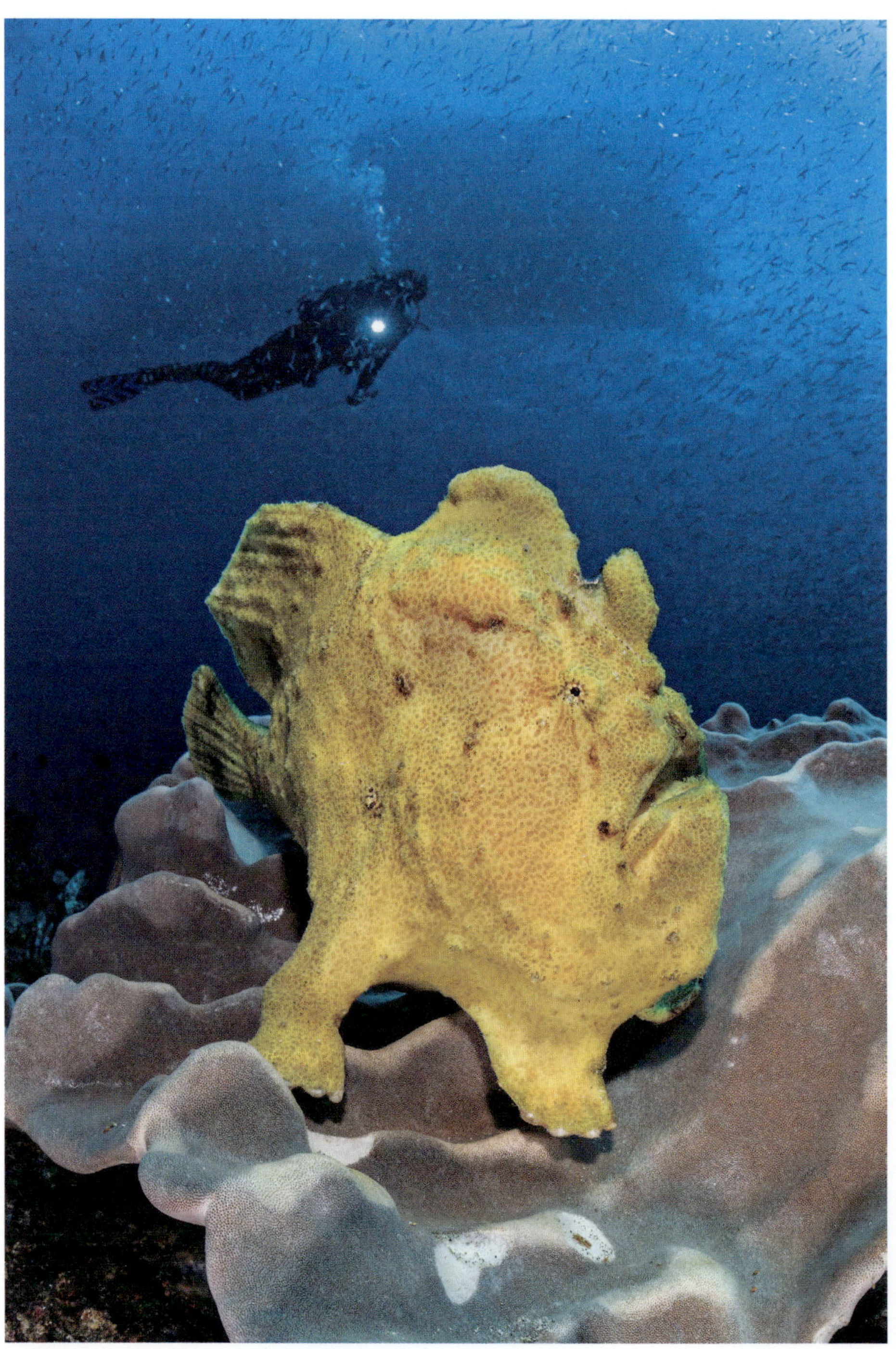

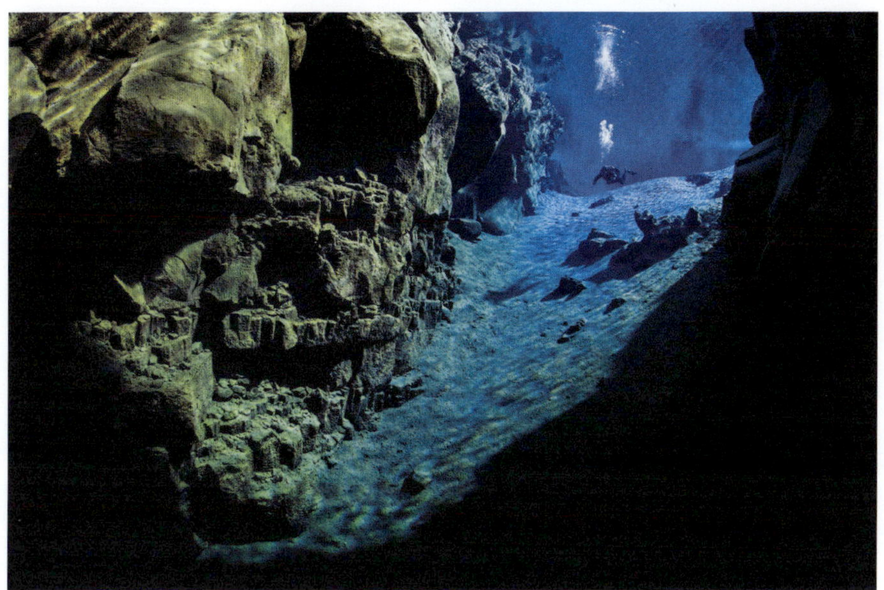

▲ Including a diver in scenic shots also adds a sense of scale to unfamiliar underwater scenery. The rift between the continental plates in Iceland is very difficult for people to understand until they see an image containing a person. With distant models, you need to make sure they are visible. Typically, you can pose them shallower, so their silhouette stands out against the brighter water surface. Here, I pressed the shutter just after my buddy breathed out, so his bubble plume helps attract the eye.

◄ Models add all-important visual depth to wideangle compositions. They are especially useful when you find a great subject, like this yellow giant frogfish, in a location without any potential for a natural background. Models are often given a flashlight because the light source makes them more visible in the picture, as well as giving their hands something to do. If the current is running, remember it is much easier for the model to swim into it. They will look more elegant too.

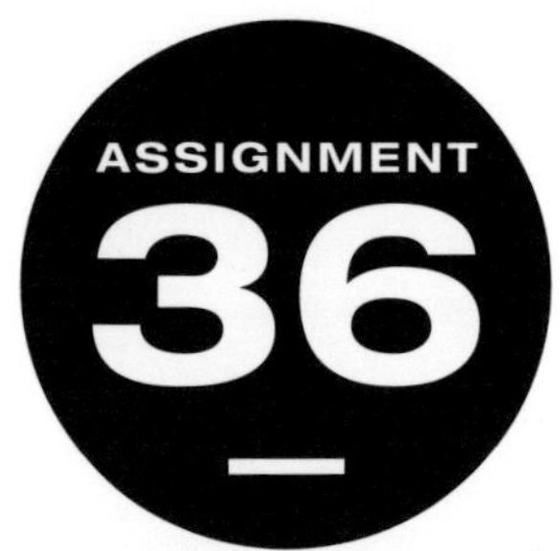

 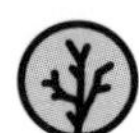

 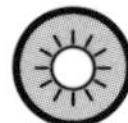

TIPS

- I regularly travel with a color-coordinated rash vest and mask to brighten images that include a model.

- When shooting wideangle scenes with models, I often shoot from the hip (see Assignment 4). Looking over the top of the camera makes it easier to check small details, such as eyelines, than it would be through the viewfinder.

LIGHT A MODEL

People pictures are important to take because they tell stories, add human interest, and give a feeling of "that could be me." A viewer's connection with the diver in the picture is strongest when we light them up, especially when the eyes are clearly visible. For this assignment, I want you to beckon your model closer, so that they are not a silhouette, but a fully illuminated part of the picture.

Your focus is getting the details right. First, make sure all the diver's gear is configured correctly and clipped in place, so nothing is dragging on the seabed. Black dive gear is fashionable, but a few splashes of color will lift your shot. A colorful rash vest, worn over the wetsuit, is an easy solution. Don't shoot while the model is breathing out, as their bubbles will obscure their face like a bushy beard. If they have long hair, keep them moving; if they stop, it will float up vertically. You can tie long hair, but it is more interesting floating free. Direct the model to move forward slightly before you shoot, which swashes their hair back off their face.

A model's eyes are arguably the most important element of these shots. You don't usually want the model staring down the lens, but because they are wearing a facemask, they need to be turned toward the camera or you won't be able to light their face. The best advice you can give is to "face the camera but look at the subject." If they are the main subject, direct them to look slightly above and to the left or right of the camera. A mask that has a single window (rather than separate ones for each eye) and a clear silicon skirt will be more flattering and is easier to illuminate without shadows. Review the images carefully and cull aggressively, keeping only those shots where these details are spot on.

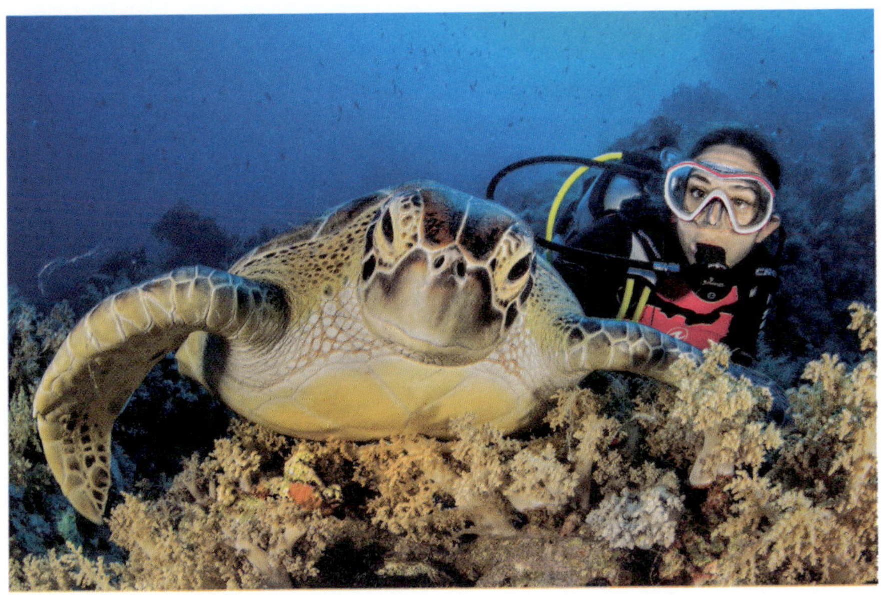

▲ It is easier to set up shots with non-moving subjects, but it is always worth trying with any moving ones you encounter, which will create memorable shots.

▼ Direct your model to face the camera, so you can light into the mask, but to look at the subject for a better story, rather than looking at the lens.

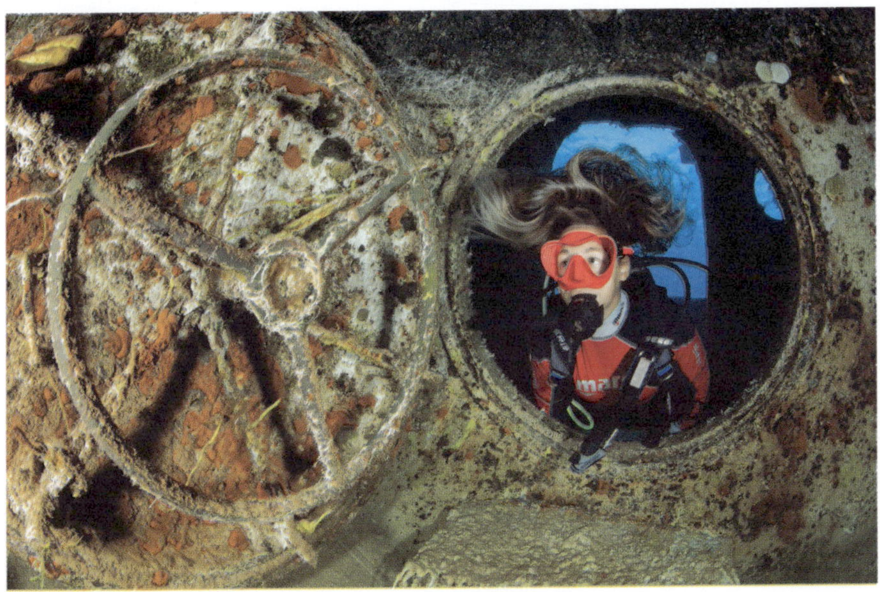

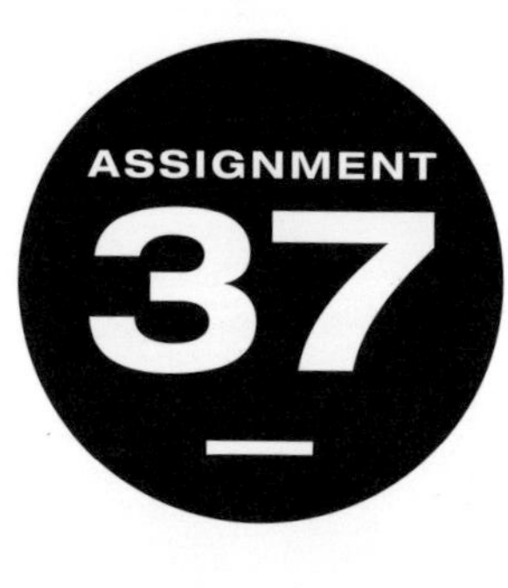

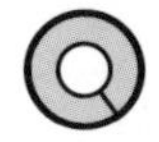
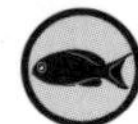
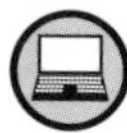

TIPS

- Unlike human faces, fish faces are streamlined to move through the water. For most species, there is no benefit in using the kind of uneven lighting used for studio portraits of people. Soft, even illumination works best with fish.

- Fish eyes are set back from the tip of their faces, so use Single-point or Eye-detection mode so your camera's autofocus locks onto an eye and not the tip of the snout.

- You can sometimes get a fish to look at the camera by waggling your finger or tapping on your housing. This only works once and only works when you stay completely still for over a minute beforehand.

DOUBLE EYE CONTACT

Fish have two eyes, but because their eyes are on the sides of their heads, it is quite rare to find a species that gives good double eye contact. Yes, you can easily take a photo where both eyes are visible, but shots where both eyes really connect with the viewer are special. Your challenge for this assignment is to find the right subject and make head-on images with a fish that gives double eye contact.

A head-on angle injects so much character into fish portraits because it arranges their features similarly to our faces, with two eyes above a nose and mouth. In turn, this allows our brains to project personality onto the subject. The result is that your picture is elevated from being a simple shot of a fish to a true portrait evoking emotion in the subject, and usually the viewer.

Finding the right species is critical. Start your search online, looking through fish pictures and noting down common species that give double eye contact. You'll find the same species come up again and again and these should become your targets. Predators often have forward-facing eyes to give them the binocular vision they need to catch their prey. The same is true of plankton-picking species, such as anthias, which need to snare tiny floating morsels. Another example is fish with flat faces and eyes that can rotate forward, like many blennies and gobies. Remember that eyes can move, so timing is critical for optimum eye contact.

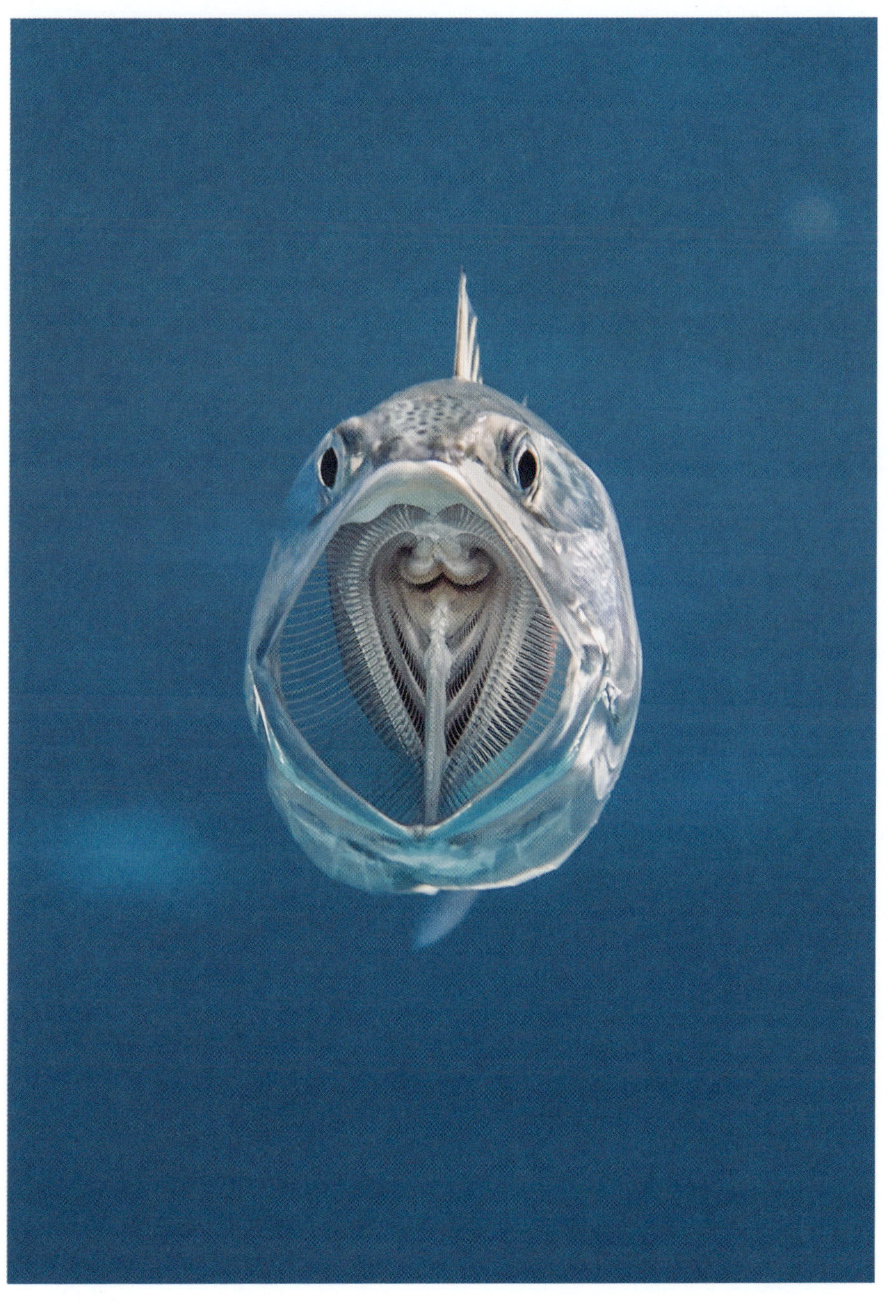

▲ *Head-on fish connect more strongly as characters with the viewer.*

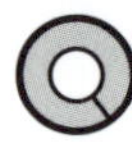

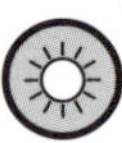

TIPS

- A narrow beam makes backlighting easier to control, so use a beam restrictor on backlighting strobes.

- Backlighting takes some time to set up. I always configure my lighting on a stone that is a similar size to the subject.

- Use back-button focus to fix focus when setting up, so you know that if the subject is in focus, it will also be in the light.

▼ *It is often the scene rather than the subject that looks great with backlighting. Here, the backlight has created a golden glow from the kelp behind this lumpsucker.*

▶ *Try backlighting on lots of different subjects. Start with only backlight and then add front fill. Decide which technique and subjects work best when you review.*

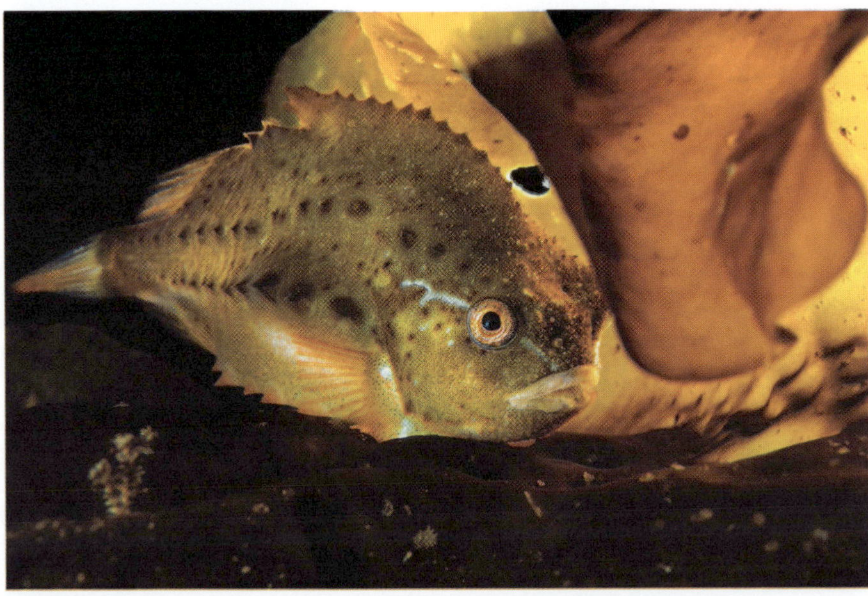

MACRO BACKLIGHT

The aim of this assignment is to see the transformative effect of backlighting on macro subjects and scenes. The best approach is to commit to backlight for entire dives, getting your setup right and then trying it on multiple subjects. You can shoot with just backlight, or you can mix it with front fill. Smaller, transparent subjects tend to suit backlight only, while more solid creatures tend to work better with some fill. It is often the habitat that is enhanced most with backlight, such as a feathery hydroid or a translucent kelp blade, and you are likely to add fill for the actual subject.

You can create backlight either by using a separate light source, such as an off-camera flash, or more simply by stretching out at least one strobe arm so that your light source is beyond the subject and can light the back of it. The key to backlighting is that the source of the light is hidden from the camera. If the subject is big enough, the light can be positioned directly behind it, but with most macro creatures this isn't possible, so you must position the light off to one side or above or below. This will still give a strong backlighting effect if the back side of the subject is illuminated.

Backlighting doesn't enhance every subject, and you will quickly determine which of your regulars it suits. It looks dramatic against a black background, so choose a subject you can frame against open water. Feathery, hairy, or translucent scenes, subjects, or parts of creatures, such as fins, look particularly good. Download and evaluate which subjects work best backlit and prioritize these on future dives.

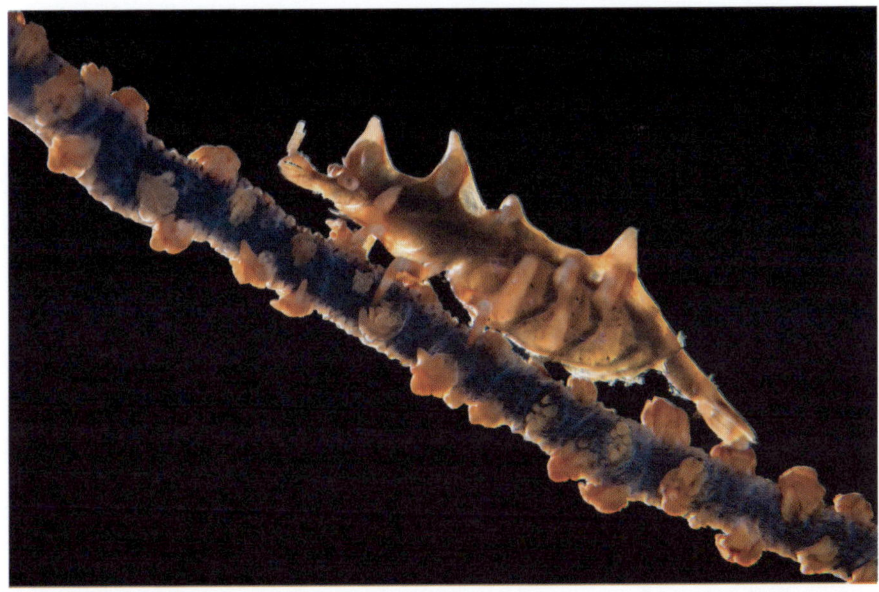

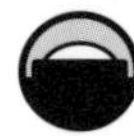
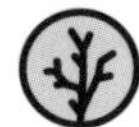

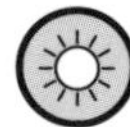

TIPS

- In Lightroom, increase the contrast and adjust the white balance to reveal the richest fluorescent colors.

- Use a small dome port and fisheye lens to get the camera and lights close.

- Strobe positions don't matter much—you are not photographing reflected light and you won't get backscatter. Pull them close and point them at the corals.

WIDEANGLE FLUORESCENCE

Shooting fluorescence underwater is a popular macro technique but is rarely used with wideangle lenses. Your challenge for this assignment is to change that! Fluorescence is commonly confused with bioluminescence, as both are common underwater, but they are completely different. Bioluminescence is the production of light by an organism, as seen when you turn off the lights on a night dive and wave your hands through the water. Fluorescence can't be seen without a light source because it occurs when a subject absorbs light at one wavelength and emits it at another. Fluorescence is most easily seen and photographed at night.

The setup for shooting fluorescence is to fit strong blue filters to your flashes to excite the fluorescence and then to add a yellow barrier filter to your macro lens to block the blue light and only allow non-reflected light through to the sensor. Many marine species fluoresce, but for this assignment, focus on corals, as they are big and are transformed from grays and browns into a rainbow of hues. Nobody makes barrier filters for wideangle lenses, but you can cut a small square of strong yellow lighting gel swatch to fit to the filter holder on the rear of most wideangle lenses.

Fluorescence photography needs lots of light, especially because the most interesting colors come from corals that fluoresce more subtly, rather than those that glow a bright green. Run your strobes on full power and push the ISO up to around 1,000 to make sure you get bright images. Also experiment with long exposures to burn in background detail revealed by artificial lights, such as those from a resort. These other light sources will have a color cast from the barrier filter, which can be corrected in processing.

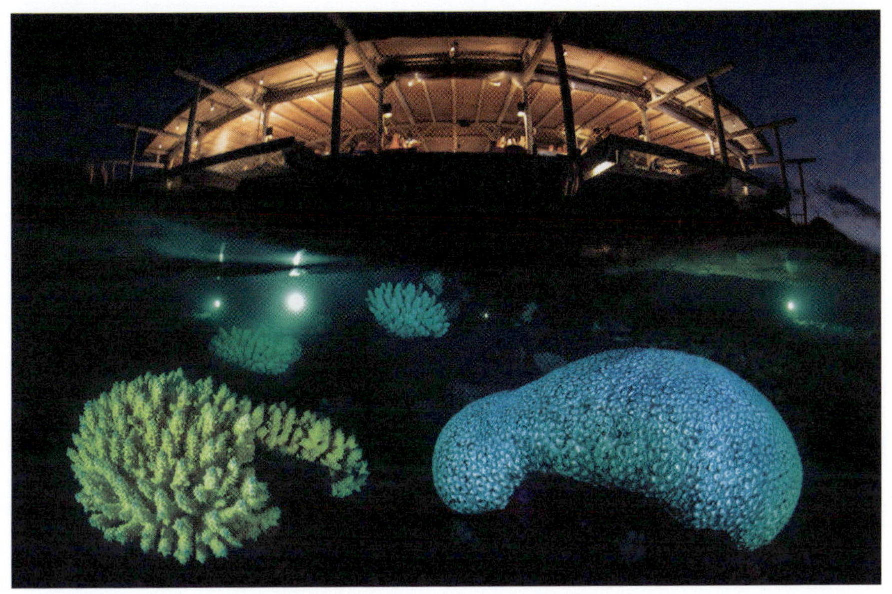

▲ *Including other light sources in the shot creates depth. The background here has both underwater spotlights and the resort lights creating background interest.*

▼ *On their own, fluorescence shots can be a little one dimensional, so consider tiling several frames together to show the diversity of colors of reef corals.*

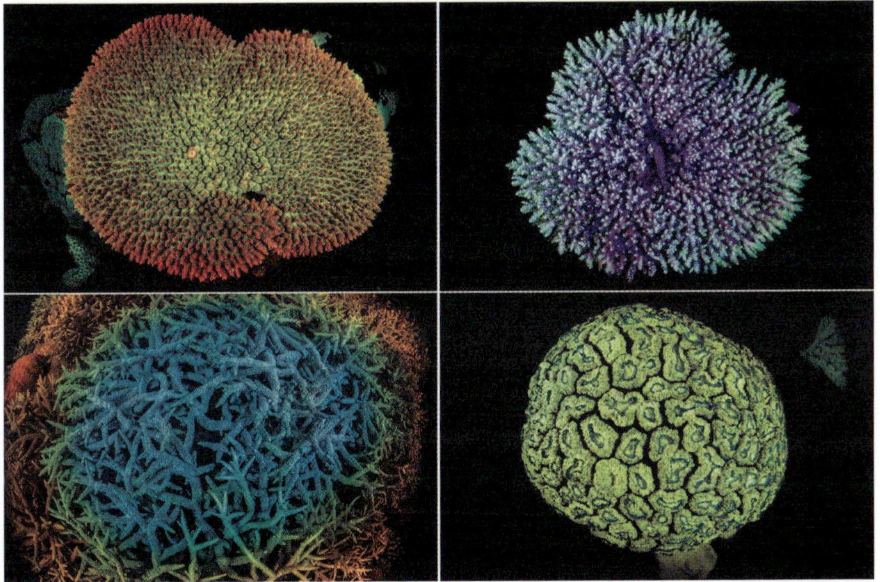

40

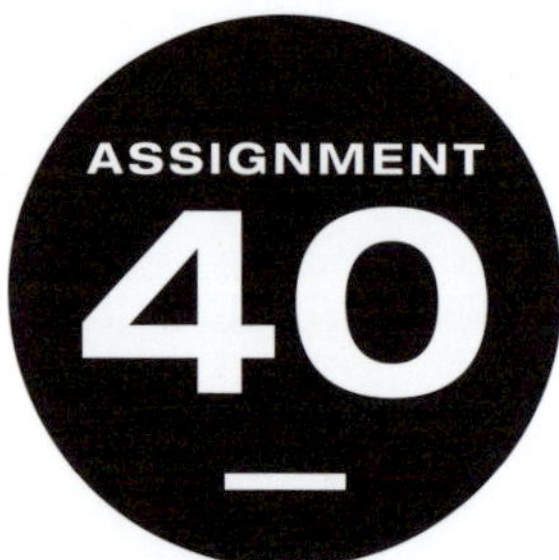
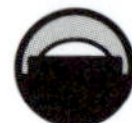 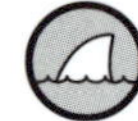
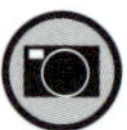

TIPS

- Set your camera to front or first-curtain sync, which is the standard flash mode on most cameras, so that the flash fires at the start of the long exposure.

- Start by panning with the subject, shoot when the composition is perfect so the flash freezes the subject, and then immediately accelerate, smoothly panning faster than the subject is moving to create the blur and a natural sense of movement.

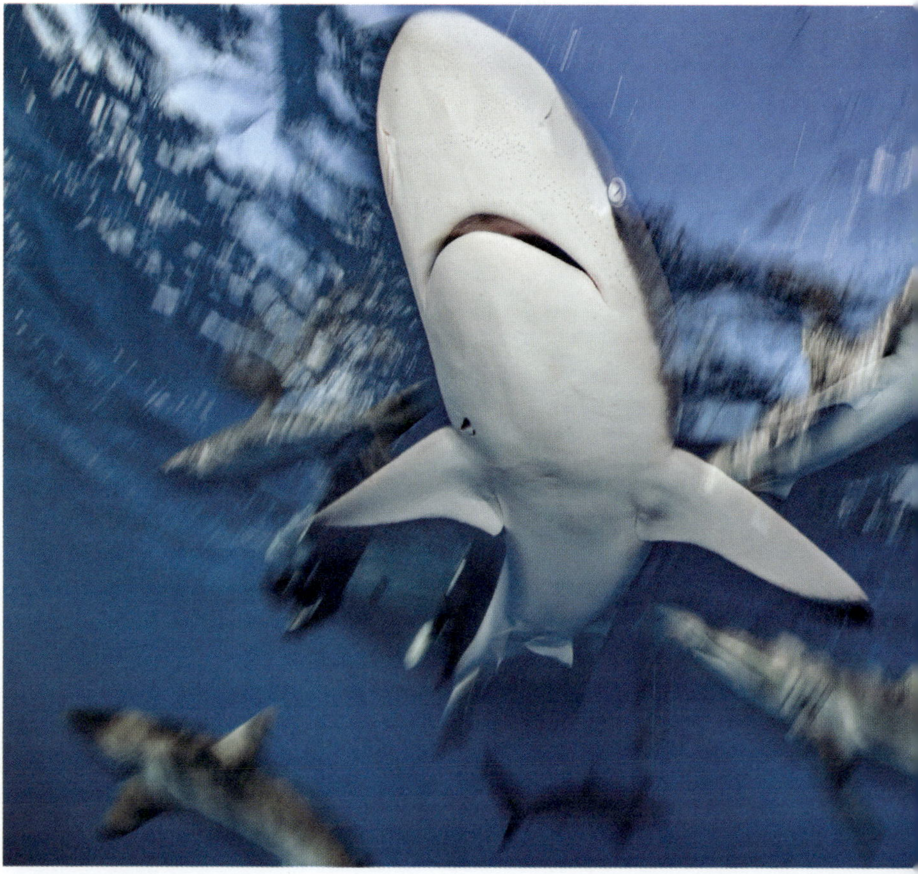

PAN-TASTIC

Capturing a sense of movement relies on the relationship between sharpness and blur, both of which look better when in the presence of the other. In this assignment, I want you to try my favored technique for creating blur in wideangle images—accelerated panning—to produce dramatic action shots. This technique has two big advantages. First, because the flash fires at the start of the exposure, the sharp portions of the frame can be precisely composed and will be reliably in focus. Second, because the camera is moved relatively quickly, the technique generates lots of blur without excessively long exposures. Accelerating past the subject also ensures that the subject blurs backward, showing a natural sense of movement.

Your goal is to use movement to add drama, energy, and atmosphere to pictures. Accelerated panning works best between shutter speeds of 1/15 sec. and 1/4 sec. Faster gives little blur; slower and the blur becomes less controllable. However, you can't simply dial in these shutter speeds—you need to drop the ISO and close the aperture so that these slow shutter speeds still give the correct ambient light exposure. Alternatively, you can wait for darker conditions, such as at the ends of the day or when it is raining.

Shoot a range of subjects against a range of backgrounds, and examine your results to appreciate how the best shots need both subject and background to work. The best subjects are typically dynamic species, such as sharks, schooling fish, and sea lions, that feel natural when shot with movement. Typically, underwater photos look best with uncluttered backgrounds, but with panning shots you need detail in the background to create movement streaks in the pictures.

◄ *Silky sharks swarm around the camera. Panning adds energy and impressionistic textures to the photo.*

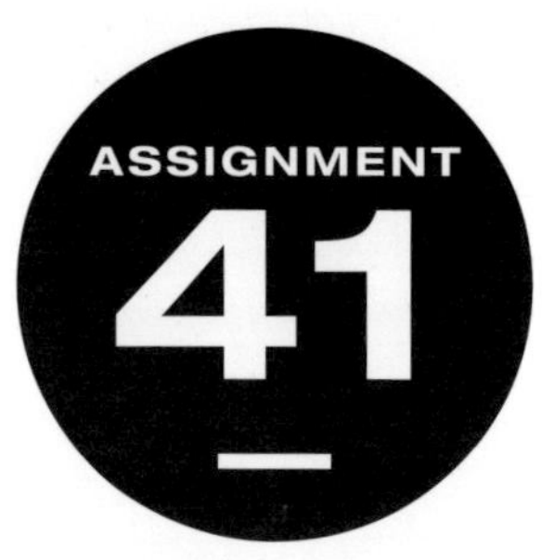

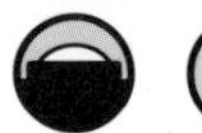
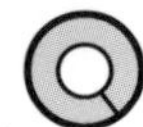
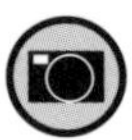

TIPS

- On the first afternoon of a trip, shoot reef backgrounds as silhouettes and keep them on the memory card. These can be combined with suitable foregrounds, macro or wideangle, when you find them.

- A few camera models do not allow double exposures. Try to borrow a camera from a friend if yours does not. Alternatively, you can combine shots in Photoshop, although this lacks the magic of doing it in-camera.

DIGITAL DOUBLES

In the film era, it was almost impossible to win an underwater photo contest with a standard exposure, such was the impact of shooting double exposures, where two pictures are photographed on top of each other to create an impossible and exciting frame. It is a technique that has fallen from fashion, but I want you to lead the revival in this assignment. The good news is that this technique is far less fiddly with a digital camera, as most, but not all, have multiple-exposure and image-overlay modes. This is a good technique to try, not just because it produces unique and creative images, but also because it rewards great precision with composition and technique.

The aim is to produce a wide range of multiple-exposure images, so this is an assignment that you might dip in and out of over a long period. The classic use of a double exposure underwater is shooting a vertical image that combines a macro foreground with a wideangle background. The macro subject is positioned in the lower half of the frame with a black background, while the wideangle background is shot in available light, mostly in silhouette, with light in the top half of the frame. The two shots are usually taken on separate dives because of the need to change lenses, then combined in-camera to create a new Raw file. Start with this technique.

Two popular variations are done using the same lens for both shots, so they can be completed on the same dive. First, with a wideangle lens, shoot an attractive foreground against black, then combine it with a silhouetted background. This is often used in areas where good subjects live too deep to be naturally framed with the surface. Second, with a macro lens, shoot a subject against black and then shoot an interesting background, such as bokeh blobs.

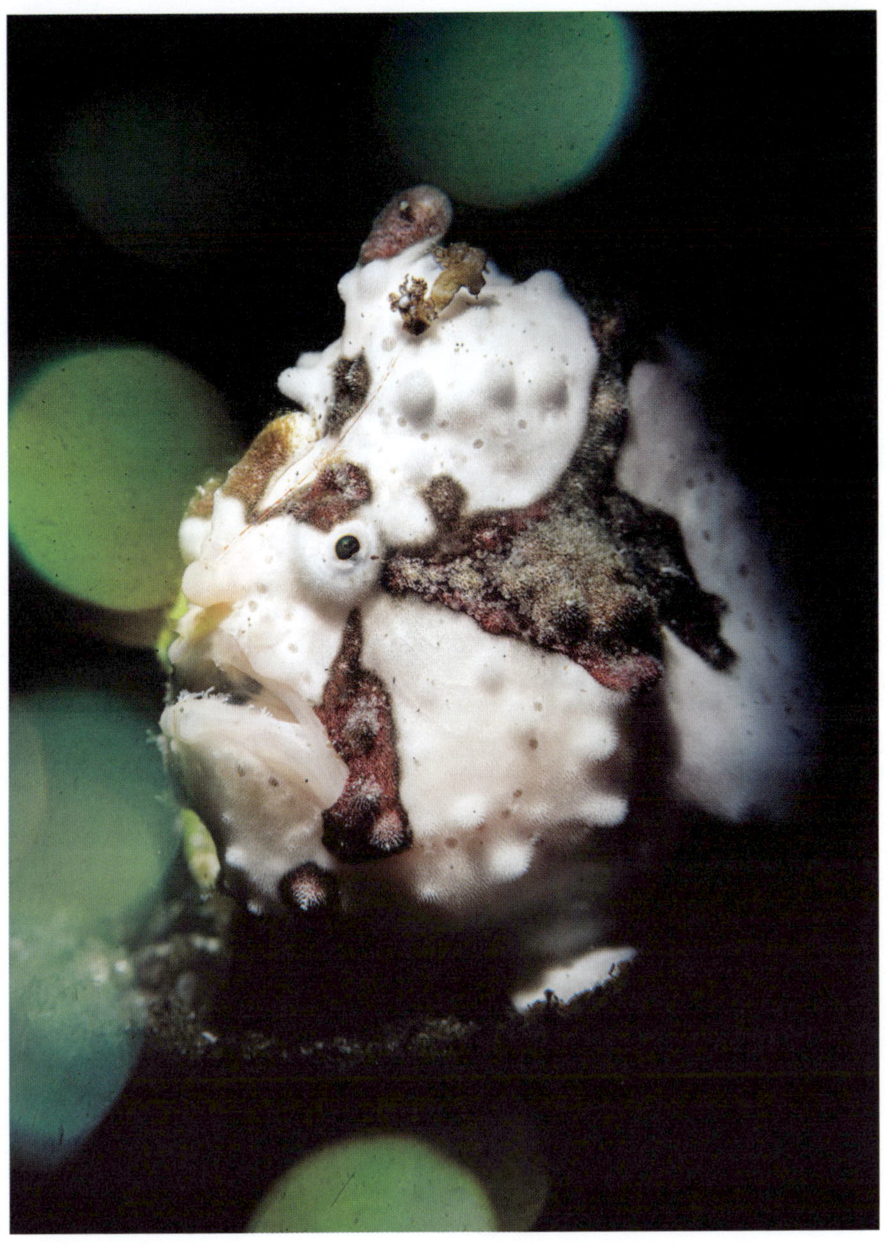

▲ *This frogfish was lit with a snoot and combined in-camera with a second exposure of out-of-focus blobs of light created by the sunlight on the underside of the surface.*

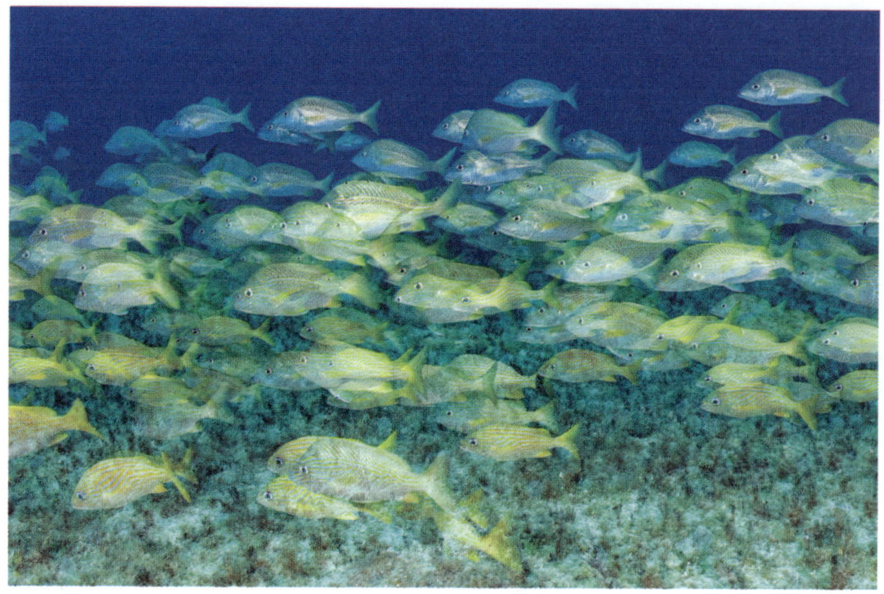

▲ *Try shooting multiple exposures of schooling fish, where each multiplies the number of fish and creates a painterly effect from the overlaying textures.*

▼ *A different technique is to start by shooting a silhouetted subject with an overexposed background. Shoot a second frame that will fill the silhouette in the double exposure.*

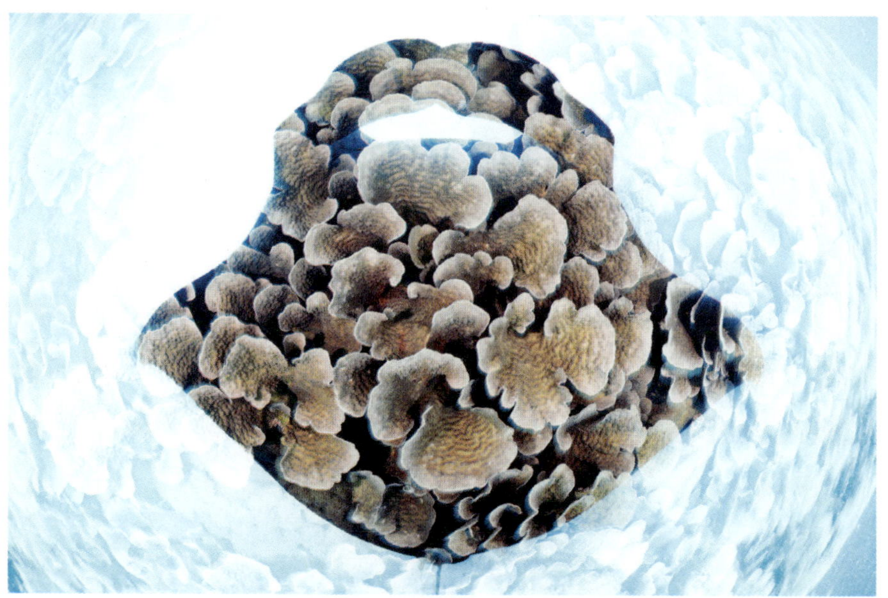

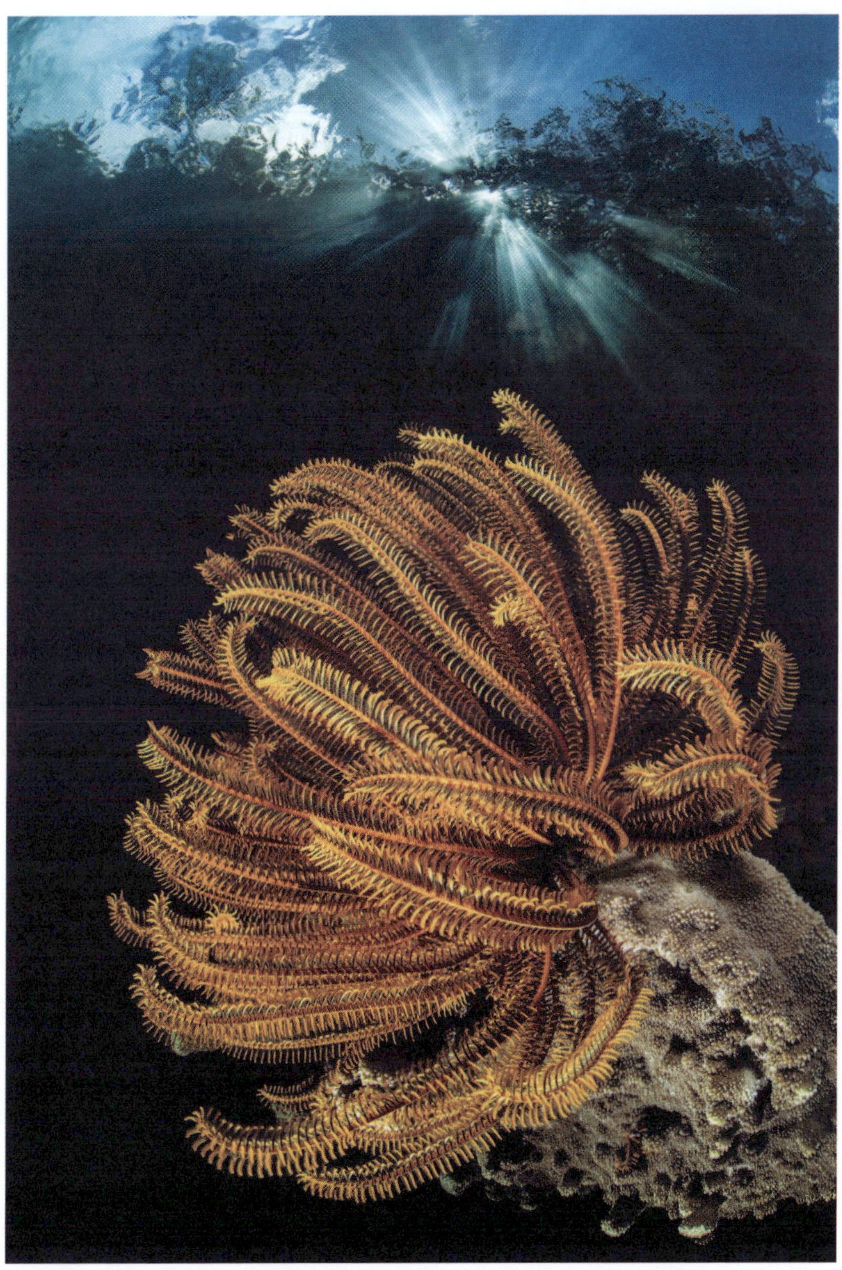

▲ *Double exposures can also be used more subtly. This shot could be a straight shot, but in this case, there were no good subjects close enough to the beautiful light coming down through the trees, so I shot the crinoid deeper as a double exposure.*

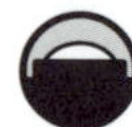

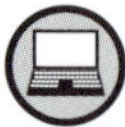

TIPS

- Reduce the ISO and close the aperture to ensure you still have the correct exposure for the water when using a long exposure.

- Zoom blur is always centered in the frame, so consider cropping asymmetrically to create a variety of compositions.

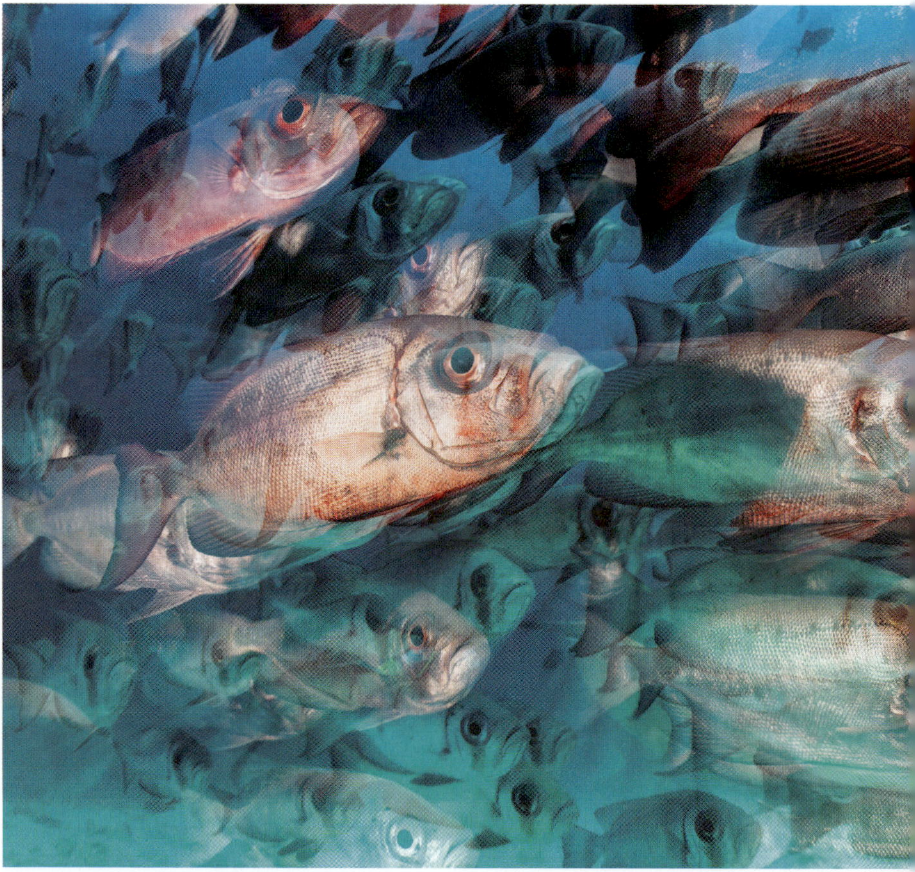

ZOOM BLUR

If you have ever dived on the face of a coral reef in a brisk current, you will have undoubtedly been mesmerized by the density and vigor of life—it is a true assault on the senses. The aim of this assignment is to learn a technique that communicates that overwhelming natural energy.

The settings for underwater zoom blurs are very similar to those for panning (see Assignment 40). First, you need a long exposure—slower than 1/15 sec. but faster than 1/4 sec. And you need the camera set to standard front-curtain sync. During the exposure, smoothly zoom the lens swiftly from wide to tight. The flash freezes the scene at the start of the exposure, and as you zoom in, the subject grows bigger on the sensor, creating streaks of light extending outward. Practice your zooming technique a few times before you shoot, so that you can do it quickly and simultaneously while pressing the shutter.

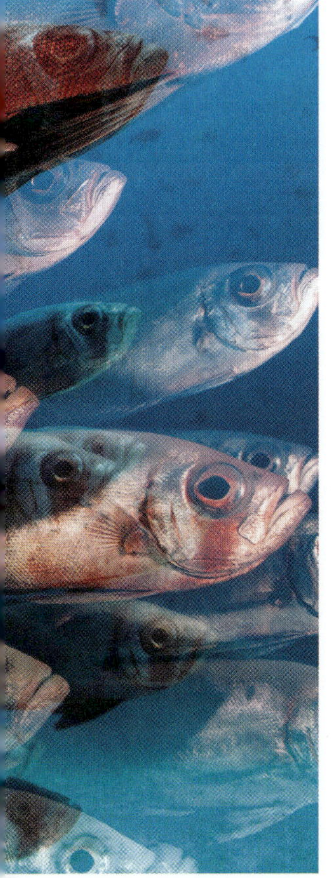

Zoom blur works best with central subjects because the blurring increases toward the edges of the frame. Spiky creatures such as corals can look particularly good, but once you have the settings dialed in, shoot lots of different subjects. This technique will work consistently, but it doesn't suit all subjects, so as part of the assignment edit your work carefully. Don't be impressed with the technique—judge the finished images on whether they work visually.

Zoom blur is also easily created in Photoshop. Simply create a new layer and apply the Radial Blur filter in Zoom mode, adjusting the center point and amount of zoom to taste. Use the Layer Mask to paint back in a sharp subject if desired. Compare your in-camera shots to your Photoshop zoom blurs and decide which you prefer. The computer gives a perfect result each time, but the in-camera shots often contain serendipitous effects that add to their appeal.

◄ I used a shutter speed of 1/13 sec. for this shot, lowering my ISO to 64 to maintain a correct exposure for the blue.

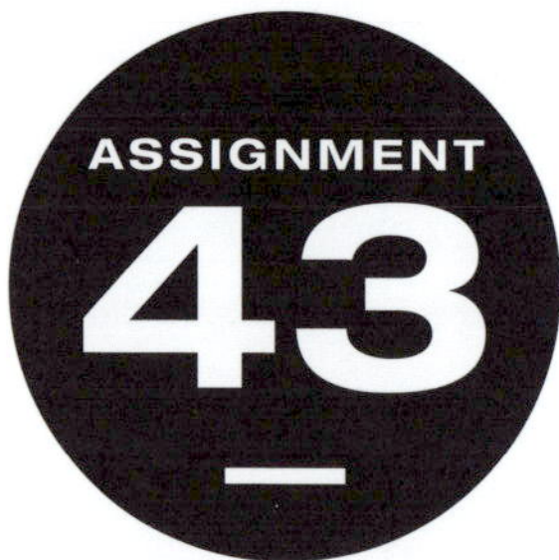

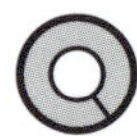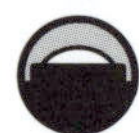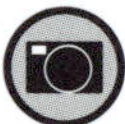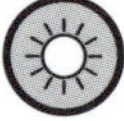

TIPS

- HSS is highly suited to shallow depth-of-field macro. If you don't have HSS, similar shots can be produced with neutral density (ND4 and ND8) filters.

- Combine HSS with wideangle lighting techniques such as crossed strobes or inward lighting to get a sharp falloff of strobe light behind the foreground.

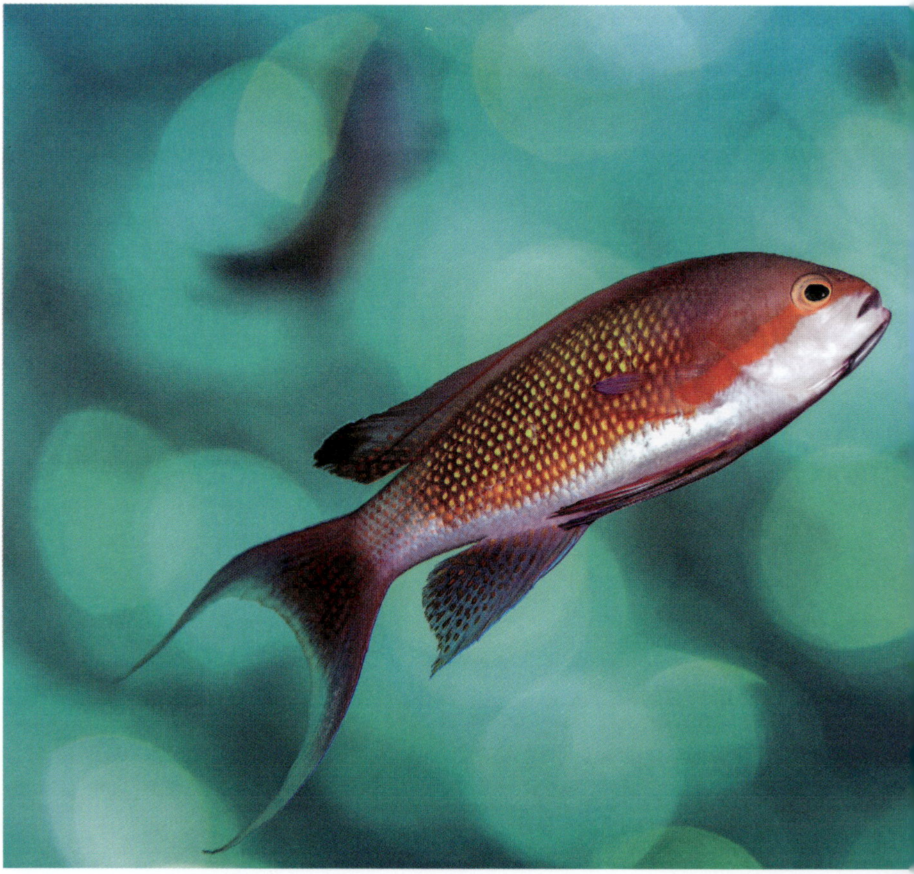

HIGH-SPEED SYNC

HSS: these three letters have been on every underwater photographer's tongue of late. They stand for high-speed sync and the last few years have seen a big increase in the number of underwater strobes featuring this capability. HSS uses clever flash protocols to fire your strobe multiple times (imperceivably fast) during an exposure, freeing you from the limitations of the camera's flash sync speed. I want you to try HSS with both macro and wideangle lenses, aiming to create images that wouldn't be possible without this new technology.

HSS is mainly used to control ambient light. For macro, this is particularly useful for shooting with an open aperture. I use HSS regularly when shooting open-aperture macro subjects into the setting sun, which creates beautiful bokeh blotches behind the subject. With wideangle lenses, you tend to use this feature to underexpose an ambient-light background. This is particularly effective for creating dark, moody images with beams of sunlight in bright shallow water.

However, HSS does have its limits, especially when shooting big scenes in bright conditions. It is common to bump up against the camera's sync speed and it is easy to think HSS is always the solution. HSS works by firing the flash twice or more during each exposure, which means it has to fire below full power, so with big scenes you can get the same result with normal sync, lowering the ISO and using the full strobe output. As soon as you shoot wideangle scenes big enough to need lots of strobe power, the ability to use HSS vanishes. Part of this assignment is finding this limit in your photography.

◀ An anthias framed against the sun, shot at f/5 to create the large blotches, which required a shutter speed of 1/1000 sec. at ISO 100.

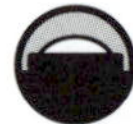
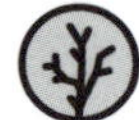
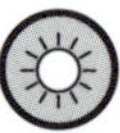

TIPS

- There is no photographic reason why we can't shoot split levels at dawn—it is just practically easier to be in the sea in the afternoon waiting for the sun to set than getting up before dawn, in a dark sea, waiting for the sun to rise.

- For lighting, push your strobes down just below the surface. A common mistake is pushing them too deep, which overexposes the seabed.

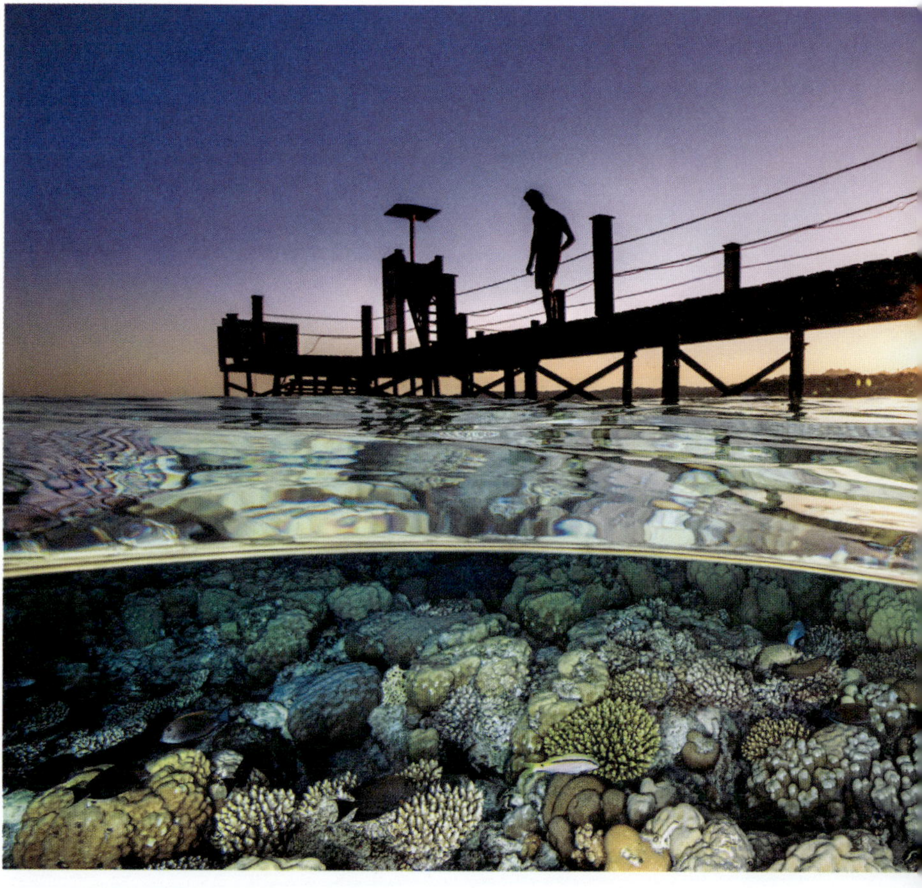

SUNSET SPLITS

For this assignment, I want you to produce one of the ultimate crowd-pleasing underwater photos: the sunset split. If a photo is worth a thousand words, a split-level photo is worth two thousand, and a sunset split turns those words into poetry. I don't want you to produce lots of different shots. Instead, dedicate your time to getting one shot exactly right. The challenge is finding the right subject matter and capturing it at a precise moment. Like a landscape photographer, channel your efforts into getting everything right, optimizing settings so that everything is correctly exposed and in focus.

To shoot a sunset split, we need subject matter in shallow water, a calm surface, and a view westward toward the setting sun. Look for subject matter shallower than 2ft (60cm) for it to be close enough to light. Lift the camera more than half out of the water and use a three-layer composition: underwater, the surface from above, and the sky. This stops you getting dark areas of reef, where the strobes can't reach into the scene.

Keep shooting until you get the perfect composition. If the sky has nice clouds, wait for the peak in their colors. If there aren't clouds, shoot at the exact moment the sun hits the horizon and creates a starburst. Droplets on the dome can be annoying and the best solution when you are in the water for a reasonable amount of time is to dip the dome, wait a second for the water surface to settle again, and shoot before the droplets form.

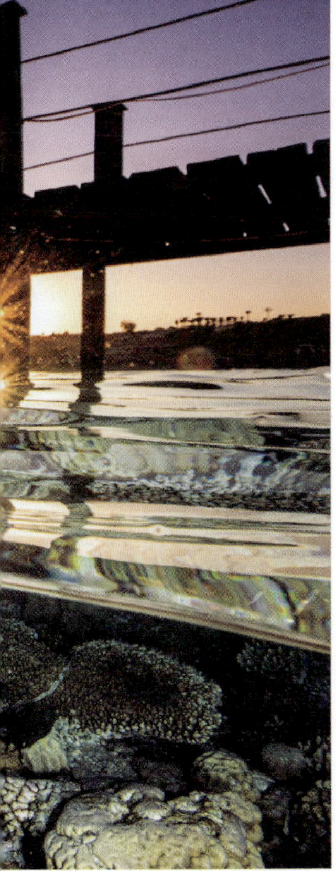

PRO TIPS

To take an attractive split-level photo, focus on the underwater subject then lock the focus. Next, shut the aperture right down to record both halves in focus and raise the ISO to 400–1,000. Use shutter speed to correctly expose the sky and adjust flash power to fully illuminate the underwater section.

◄ *Find your composition before the light peaks, set up and wait for the prime moment. You only need one shot!*

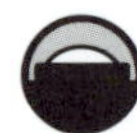
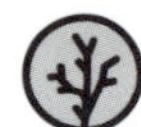

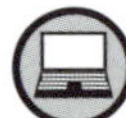

TIPS

- The main reason panoramas fail to stitch is that there is too little overlap between individual frames. When using fisheye lenses or underwater wet lenses, overlap the frames by at least 30 percent to help the stitching software.

- Always shoot lots of extra space around your intended composition. Once on land, you can easily crop a panorama, but you can't take more pictures.

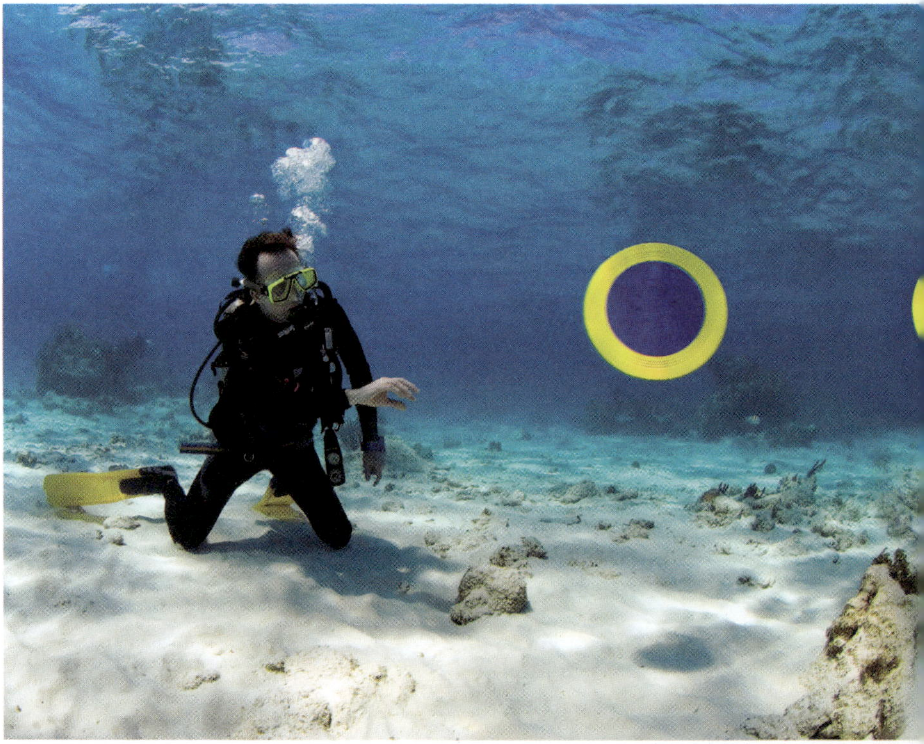

PANORAMAS

The aim of this assignment is to shoot a panoramic picture that truly fills the extended frame with a captivating composition. You will need to visualize how the scene will work before you shoot. When you've stitched your images together, assess your panorama and ensure that it is interesting and balanced from edge to edge. Don't simply judge shots based on if they are joined up correctly.

When panoramas become too elongated, they are difficult to view and use, so I usually aim for an aspect ratio of around 16:9, the same as a TV. I will often shoot five to seven vertical images when creating a horizontal panorama, but remember that you can also use the panorama technique to shoot completely square compositions or even the standard aspect ratio of your camera. Underwater photography is often limited by visibility and shooting a panorama is a powerful technique for shooting big subjects from even closer than you can with your widest lens.

▼ *Create panoramas that make the most of the picture format.*

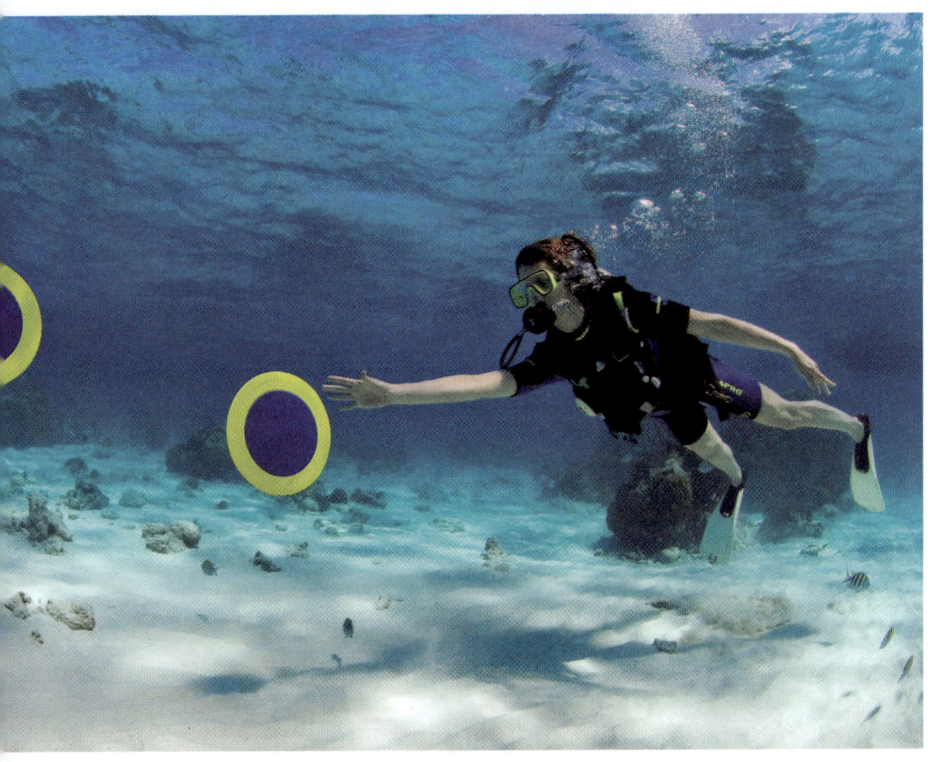

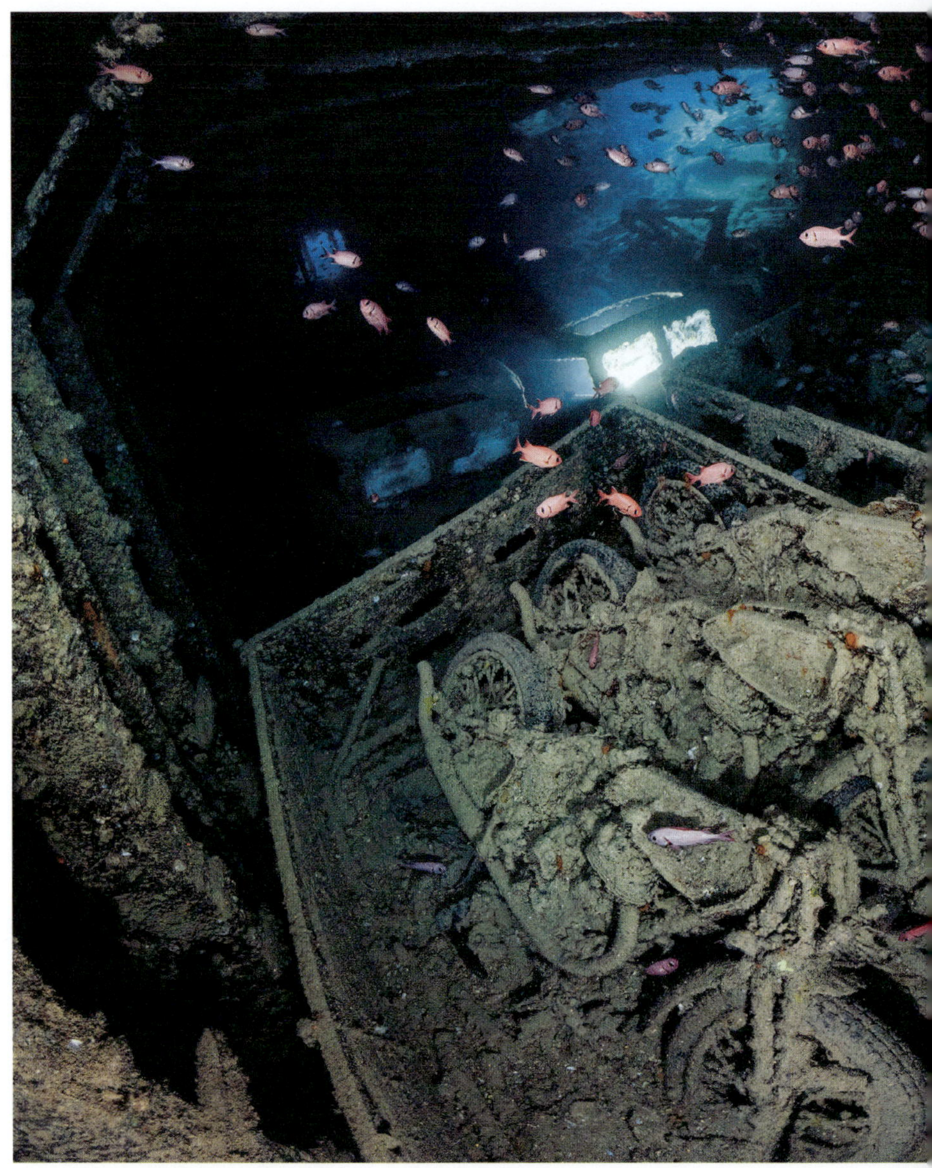

You can't use a tripod when shooting panoramas underwater. Instead, you must maintain a reasonably consistent position in the water. Use the same focus, exposure, and white balance throughout so that the images remain consistent. Take your time shooting, stopping for a moment after turning for the next frame

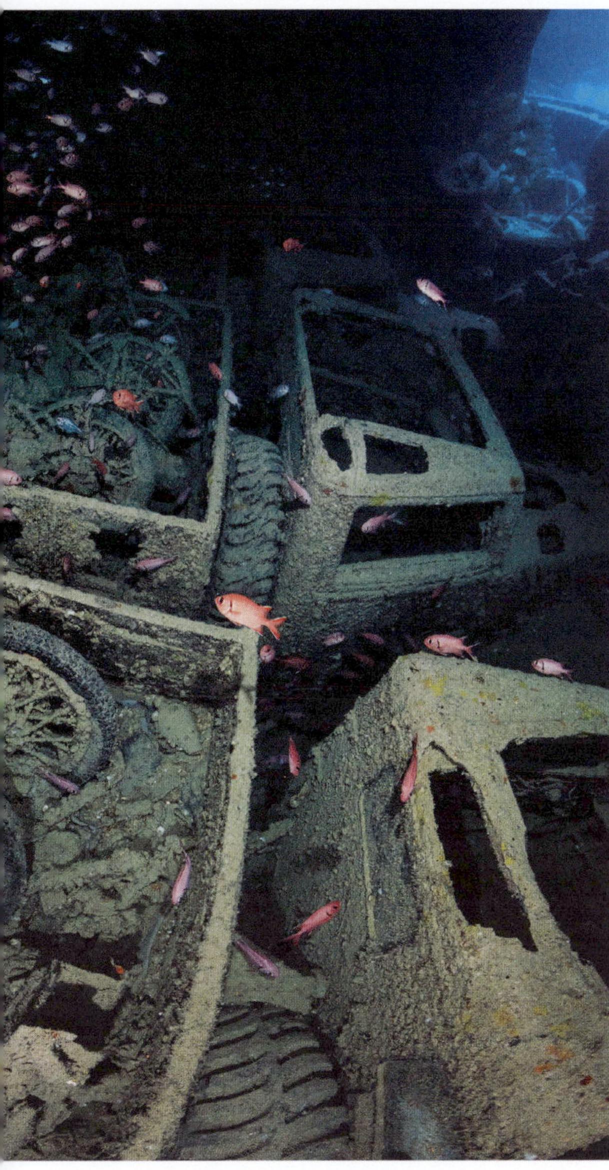

to allow the momentum of the water to dissipate, otherwise it will keep you turning and blur the picture. In shallow water, there is no need to use flash, but when in deeper water, give time for your flashes to recycle properly between shots, so that the flash exposure stays consistent.

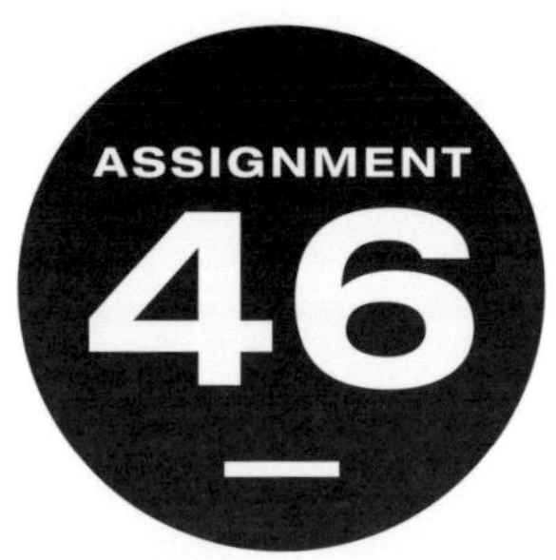

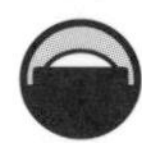

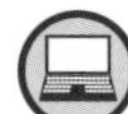

TIPS

- A statue, coral head, or sunken car can be mapped effectively with photogrammetry with as few as 50 photos with a 70-80-percent overlap. Just make sure you shoot from every angle.

- Use manual camera settings and wait for your strobes to recycle properly between each shot to keep the panorama consistent edge to edge.

- Photogrammetry software needs to know what lens you used, so avoid using accessory wet lenses that are not recorded in the EXIF. Native fisheye lenses are fine.

PHOTOGRAMMETRY

Photogrammetry is one of the most exciting recent advances in underwater photography. It is essentially a 3D scanning process, where you take tens or hundreds of overlapping photos of an object from all angles and then use specialist software to turn them into a model of the subject. The software calculates where each image was taken from and uses this information to build up the model, creating a surface with details, texture, and colors from the original pictures. Like a super-panorama, this technique is particularly useful underwater because it allows the mapping of subjects far bigger than it is possible to see in the visibility. It is regularly used by specialists for mapping shipwrecks and underwater landscapes.

Most underwater photographers have never tried this technique, so the objective of this assignment is simply to give it a go. Don't set out to map an entire shipwreck on your first attempt. Instead, look for an object in the size range of a person to a car. There are many easily accessible underwater statues around the world, and these are a highly suitable place to start.

Photogrammetry requires specialist software—I recommend 3DF Zephyr, which is PC only. This program is an industry leader and helpfully has a simplified free version. But be warned, it is an amazing process, and it is very easy to get addicted to such underwater witchcraft! I hope you do.

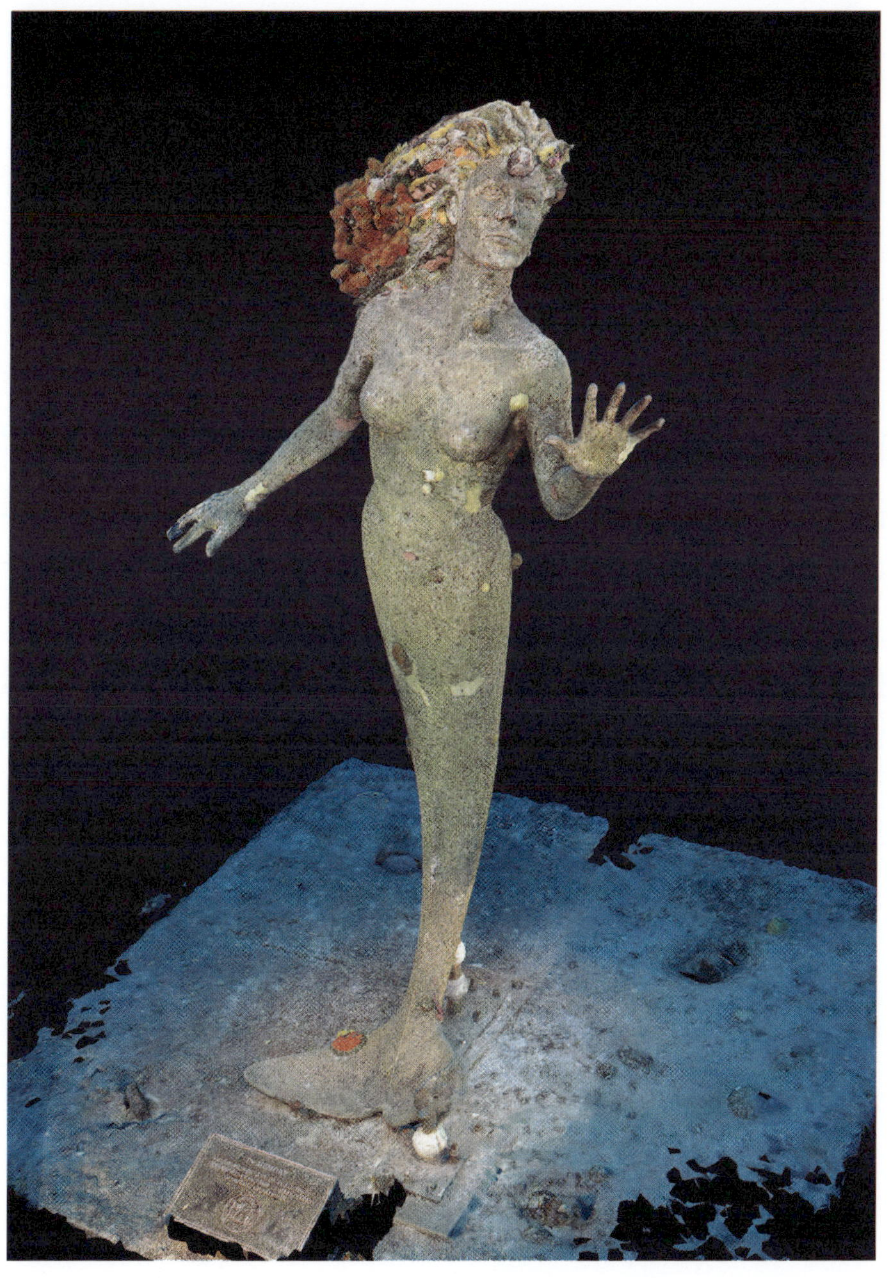

▲ *This is just one angle of the 3D model of a mermaid statue that photogrammetry built from my images.*

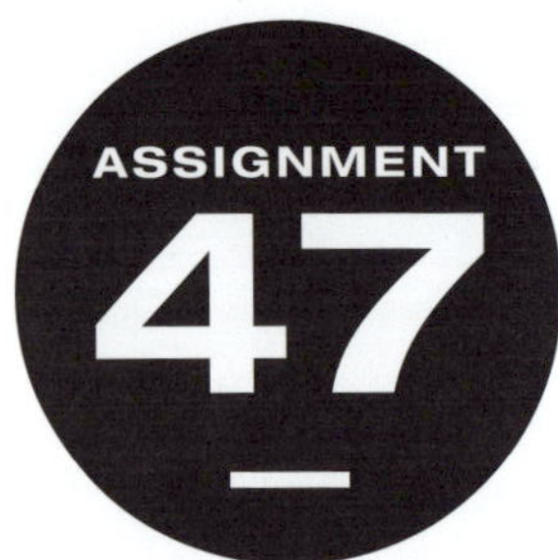

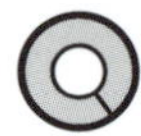
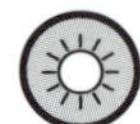

TIPS

- Focus on larger macro subjects—small subjects are less likely to take the light in interesting ways and the restricted depth of field will also be a limitation.

- Use manual exposure to keep the flashlight exposure consistent, whether the subject is large or small in the frame. Negative space is important in these pictures.

- Don't be afraid to use high ISOs for these shots, as keeping a reasonably fast shutter speed is critical for getting sharp results.

▼ *Don't simply use the flashlight in the same way as your strobe—aim to produce different-looking underwater images.*

▶ *Encourage your buddy to light from all angles. Here, the flashlight was on the seabed behind this yellow hairy frogfish.*

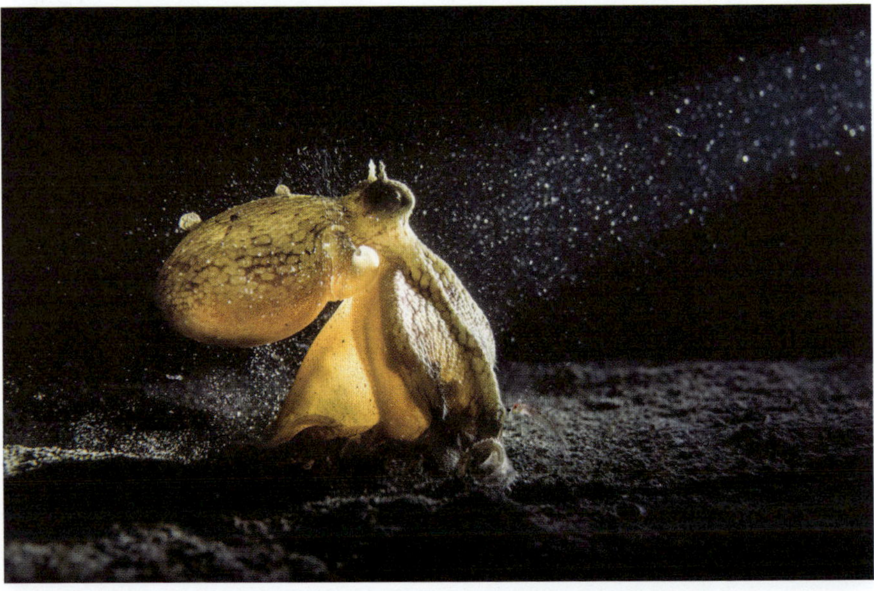

MACRO FLASHLIGHT

Most underwater photos are lit with flashes attached to the camera on strobe arms, so freeing your light source from such a restriction should uncork your creative juices. In this assignment, I want you to hand over the lighting responsibility to your buddy. This is a two-person assignment, where you should take your housing down without strobes or arms attached and give your buddy a powerful dive flashlight or video light with a focused, narrow beam. I suggest starting this assignment on a night dive, where the flashlight will be the only light source and you can use a higher ISO to keep the shutter speed at about 1/125 sec. for sharpness.

Discuss ideas for lighting before the dive and rehearse some shots by placing an object on a table and getting your buddy to walk around, lighting it with the flashlight from the front, top, side, and back. They can even restrict the beam further, by blocking parts of it with their hand, to help create interesting lighting. A few minutes' practice on land will be very valuable once you get underwater.

Your aim is to produce a range of shots from each subject as the light moves around them. If they are mid-water, try lighting from above, below, all sides, and back and front. If the subject is on the seabed, try side, back, and front, and with the light skimming across the sand onto the subject. Both photographer and lighting assistant should be contributing to the photographic process, so don't simply boss your buddy around. Revel in the variety and creativity that two heads can bring.

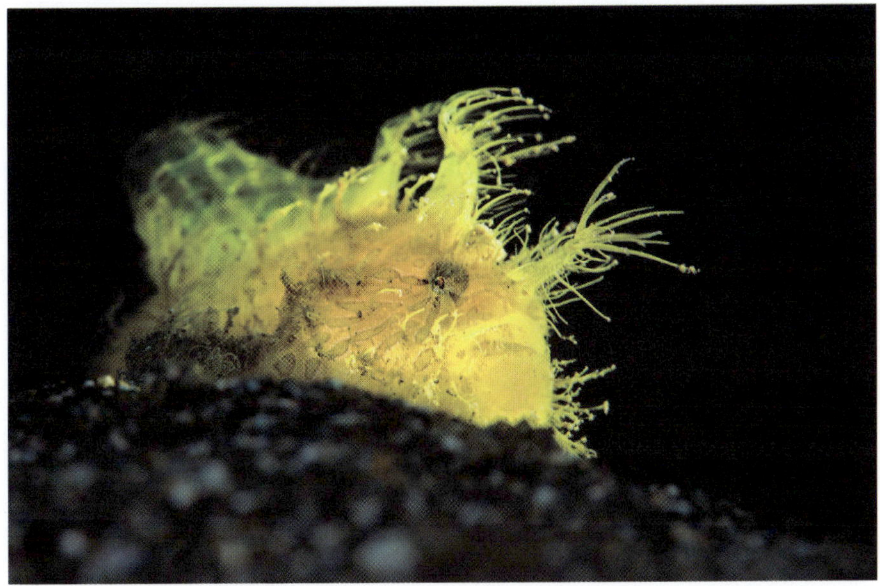

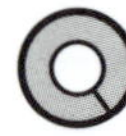

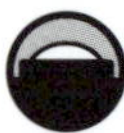

TIPS

- You don't need rare subjects or complex behaviors for special shots—a picture that captures the perfect moment will always have tremendous visual appeal.

- Start with behaviors that you are familiar with, or that play out repeatedly so that you can predict and be ready to capture the peak of the action.

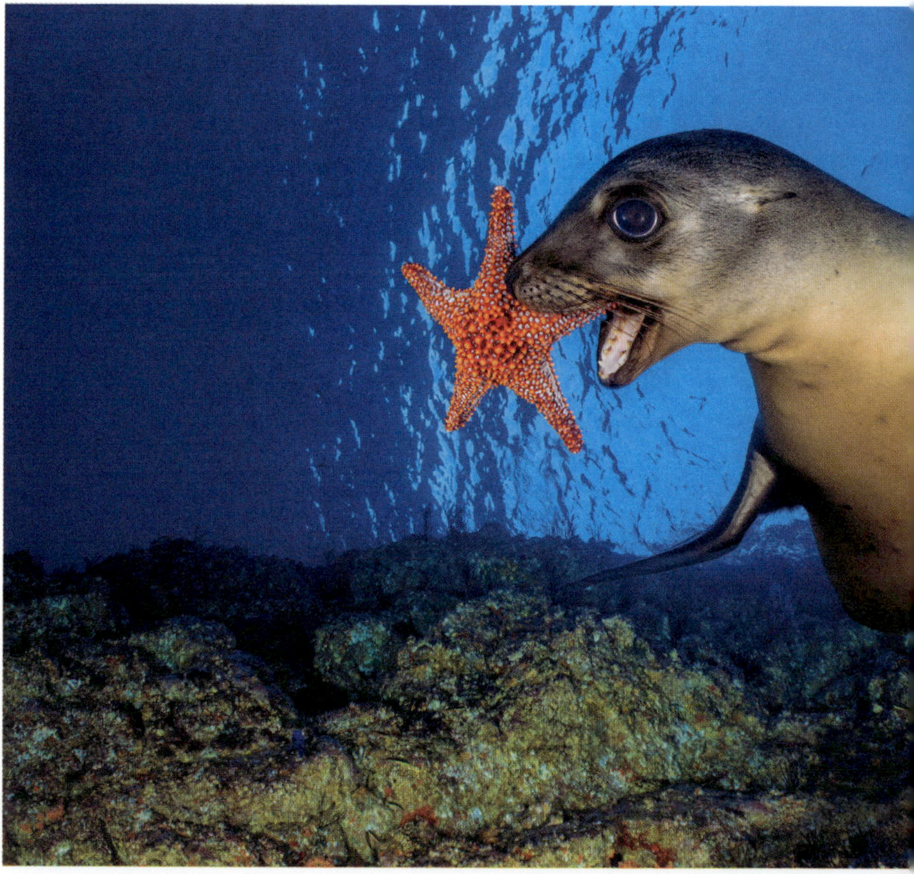

DECISIVE MOMENT

I believe that with any subject I shoot there is an optimal time to squeeze the shutter. Even with a wreck or reef scene, there are bound to be small changes in the composition happening all the time, such as fish swimming into an ideal position or a piece of kelp unfurling elegantly in the swell. Developing a sense for the decisive moment is hugely valuable for your photography, and nowhere are these lessons easier to learn than when shooting behavior.

For this assignment, I encourage you to seek out natural behavior and focus on capturing a shot at the peak of the action. You should also aim for a picture that tells the whole story in a single frame, rather than relying on a series of pictures to document what was happening.

The first step to seeing behavior underwater is diving slowly and sympathetically, so the wildlife continues to act naturally. There are many common behaviors to look for, such as cleaning, symbiosis, or egg guarding. Before rushing in to make images, take time to watch and understand. This can help you decide on what will be the decisive moment. With cleaning, for example, it is great to get shots where the cleaner is in contact with the client fish. It gets even better if the cleaner is in an interesting position, such as inside the mouth. Challenge yourself to aim for the best possible shot.

Most underwater photos require flash, and this prohibits the spray-and-pray approach. The more time we spend around a subject, the more relaxed it will become. Use this time to rehearse camera settings and lighting, so that when the moment comes you don't miss the chance to capture it. Once you have made behavior shots at the peak of the action, incorporate this mindset in all your photography.

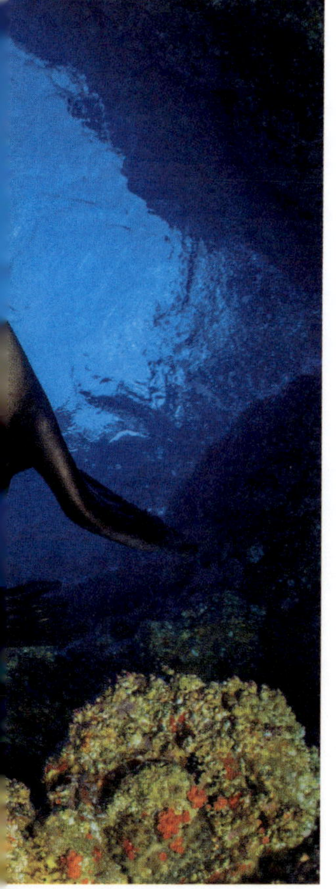

◀ *A sea lion pup plays with a starfish. I squeezed the shutter when the pup caught up and was about to grab the starfish it had dropped and was chasing.*

ASSIGNMENT 49

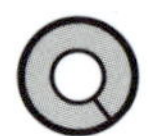 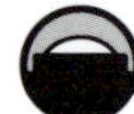

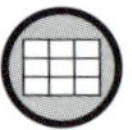

▶ *Ghost pipefish are about the size of a key, but right in front of my wideangle lens, they filled the frame. Still dissatisfied by the barren surroundings, I used the zoom blur technique (see Assignment 42) to make them more appealing.*

▼ *Naturally, I prefer my wideangle shots of turtles, but this macro image of the face definitely adds to my turtle portfolio.*

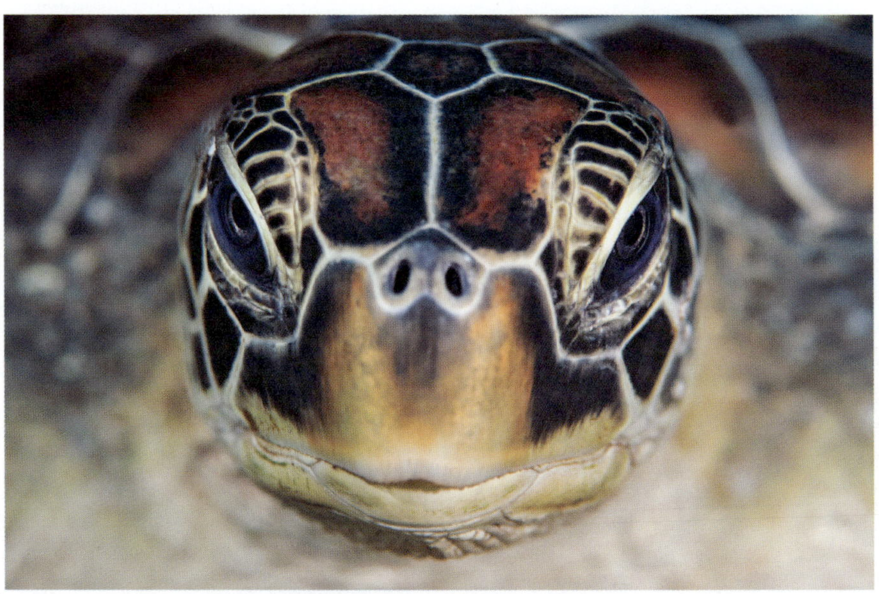

WRONG LENS

Follow the rules and you will end up with the same photos as everyone else; break the rules and you will create something that stands out. Underwater photographers can't reach into a camera bag mid-dive and so we plan our dives carefully to have the right lens for the expected subjects. Nobody goes searching for nudibranchs with a wideangle lens or visits a manta-cleaning station with a macro lens, but the challenge of this assignment is to do just that and take on a classic wideangle subject with a macro lens and vice versa. This might be an assignment you end up doing accidentally, when you encounter a great subject with the wrong lens fitted!

One advantage of shooting with the wrong lens is that they tend to emphasize size. A large creature shot with a macro lens looks big, while a small creature shot with a wideangle lens looks small. Use this to your advantage in compositions. With the former, you can focus on features like eyes, the face, or skin patterns. With the latter, focus on revealing the relationship between the animal and its environment.

The "wrong lens" approach is particularly valuable if you regularly photograph the same subjects. It is easy to get stuck in a rut, shooting everything the same way, and this assignment guarantees something different. As part of the exercise, assess the "wrong lens" photos alongside your images of the subjects taken with the correct lens. It's not about which is better, but that the alternative images will greatly increase the diversity of your coverage of the species.

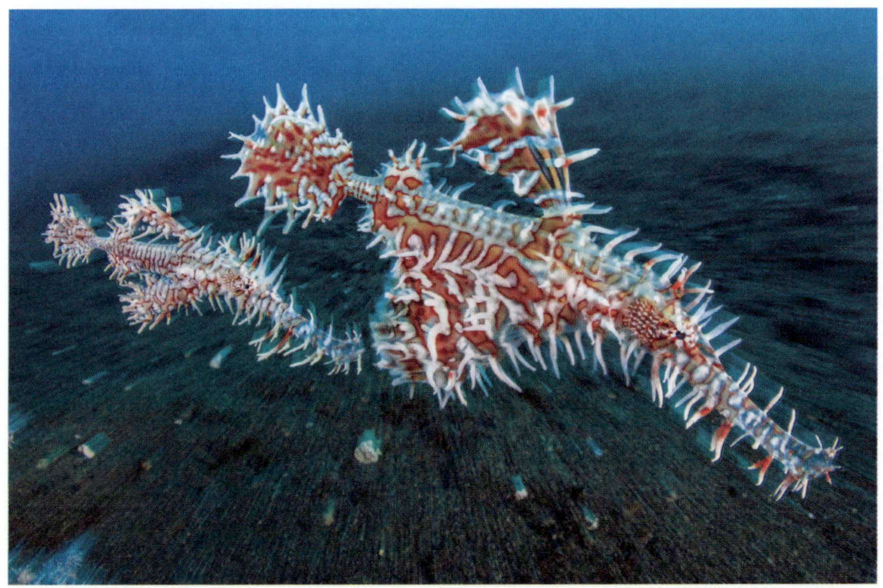

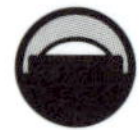
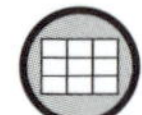
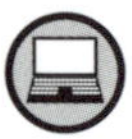

TIPS

- Cover shots have many technical requirements, but they must always represent the publication. For example, not every underwater shot works for a scuba diving magazine, so consider the subject matter as well as the format.

- Not all magazines are the same shape. In Europe, publications tend to be closer to a 3:2 aspect ratio, while in the States, many are closer to 4:3. Asian magazines are usually somewhere in the middle. Change your template shape to represent the magazines you read.

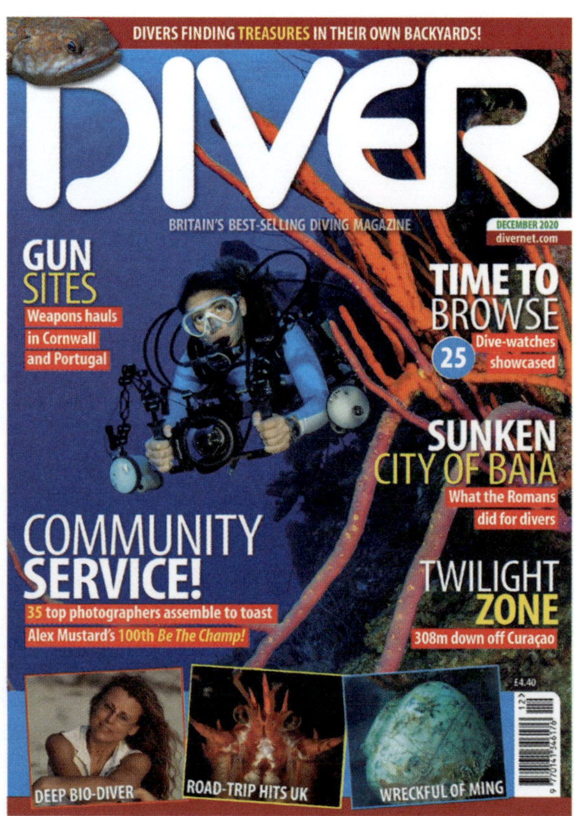

COVER SHOT

There are few sights more rewarding than seeing your photo staring back at you from the shelves of a newsstand, particularly when your picture is on the cover of a magazine that you have read for years. Cover shots need to be carefully crafted to fit unique requirements. In addition to being eye-catching, there are two golden rules: shoot vertical and leave space in the frame.

This is a two-part assignment. The first is computer based. Start by creating a magazine template in Photoshop—make a new document with a height of 4,000 pixels and width of 2,800 pixels, with the background set to Transparent. Now, use the Type tool to add a title, in a bright font, that fills the top of the frame—this is called the masthead. Next, in a smaller font, add a few cover lines down the sides, copying the look of a magazine you have around the house. If you are really keen, you can add a strapline, a top banner, and even a barcode. What you will quickly see is how little room is left for a photo.

Head to your image folder and select a few vertical images you think might be suitable covers and resize them to 4,000 pixels tall. Copy and paste one onto the magazine template. In the Layer menu, move the photo to the rear-most layer to see how it works with the text. Try a few to get a feel for the requirements. Often, some of our best compositions become too busy with all the cover "furniture" added or the text ends up covering what made the image interesting. Typically, minimalist shots work best.

The second part of the assignment is to head underwater and shoot vertical images specifically for the cover. Aim for simple compositions, strong colors, and a central subject. Different subjects suit different magazines, but the shots always need to fit the format. Keep your favorites in a Lightroom collection, as it is valuable to have suitable shots ready when a magazine comes calling.

◀ *A real magazine cover leaves little room for the photo.*

▶ *The original composition as submitted to the magazine*

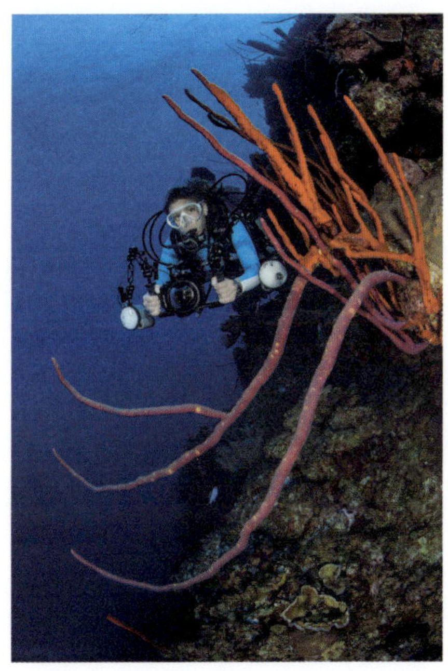

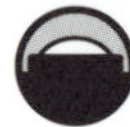
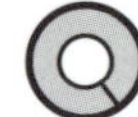
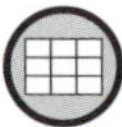

TIPS

- Pick up a good magazine and look through the big features and analyze the photos in terms of content and technical variety. Think about what lenses have been used and how compositions advance the story.

- Good photojournalism isn't about producing five contest winners, but five images that fully explore and illustrate the topic and its many nuances.

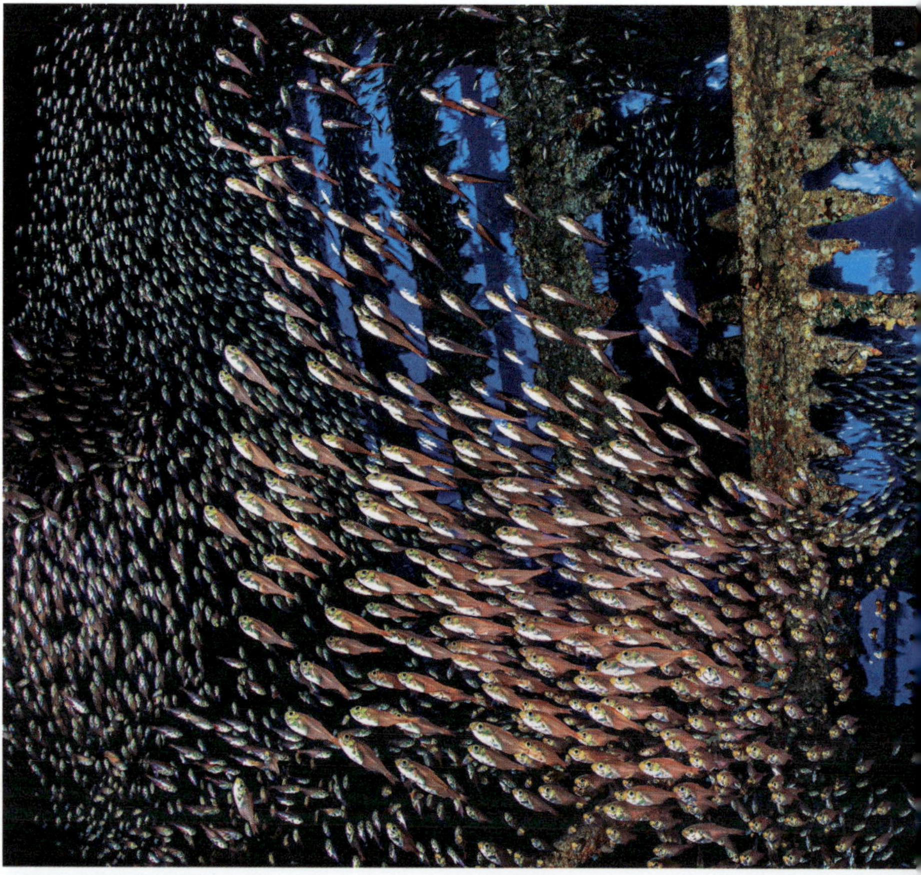

TELL A STORY

There are lots of photographers who can take a beautiful picture, but far fewer who can create images that communicate and tell a story. For this assignment, I want you to become a photojournalist and build a narrative across five images. This is likely to take several dives and utilize several different lenses and photographic techniques.

The first step is to decide on a topic. You might choose to describe a shipwreck, reveal the secrets of a species, or simply tell the story of a dive. Avoid repetition, with each image focusing on a different aspect of the story. For a wreck, you could shoot an atmospheric image, then a big shot of the bow, a close-up of an interesting artefact, some marine life living on the wreck, and a diver exploring. Shooting a nudibranch, you could start with a stunning head-on portrait, then a mating shot or egg-laying image, a hitch-hiking emperor shrimp, a wider shot showing a diver looking at the slug, and a close-up detail of rhinophore or the color pattern.

Reportage of a dive might start with a split of divers jumping in, then the reef with the boat above, divers encountering marine life, and some close-ups of marine life, and finish with divers hanging onto a safety stop. Brainstorm ideas before you dive.

A magazine designer won't use two similar images in a feature, so vary your style and approach. Shoot horizontals and verticals, macros and wideangles, silhouettes and strong colors, classic and creative techniques. That said, your images still need to be coherent, which is why top magazines typically get one photographer to shoot a story rather than buy stylistically unconnected shots from stock.

You should aim to produce more than twice the number of finished images you need and then reduce them down to the best five for the story. Remember, you are not picking for social media or contests, so select the images that advance the narrative, even if they are not your favorite standalone shots.

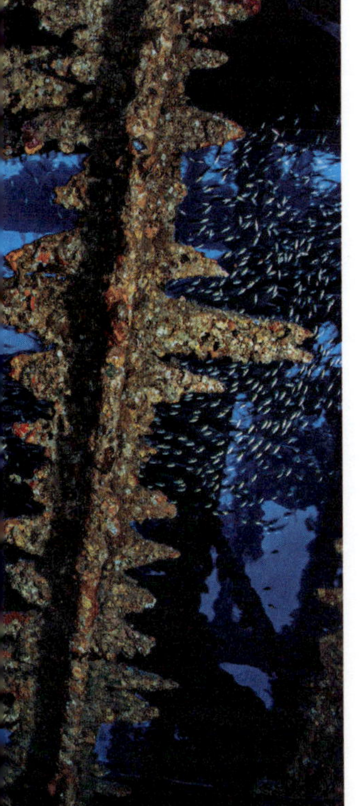

◀ *A wreck story needs more than the classic views of the ship. Diversify your collection by shooting artefacts, macro, divers, and marine life.*

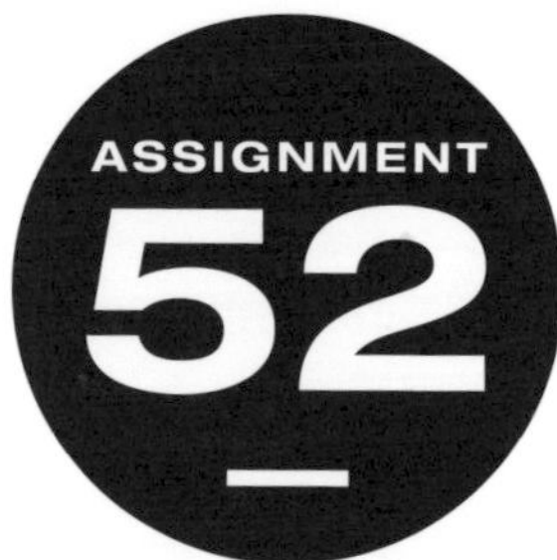

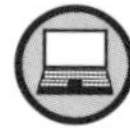
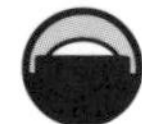
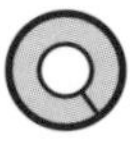

TIPS

- Photography contests regularly bring out the best in photographers, giving them a focus on excellence, but occasionally they bring out the worst, making them treat everyone else, even their subjects, as the opposition. Always be respectful.

- Take your photography seriously, but remember that judging is subjective, and keep a level head whether you win or lose.

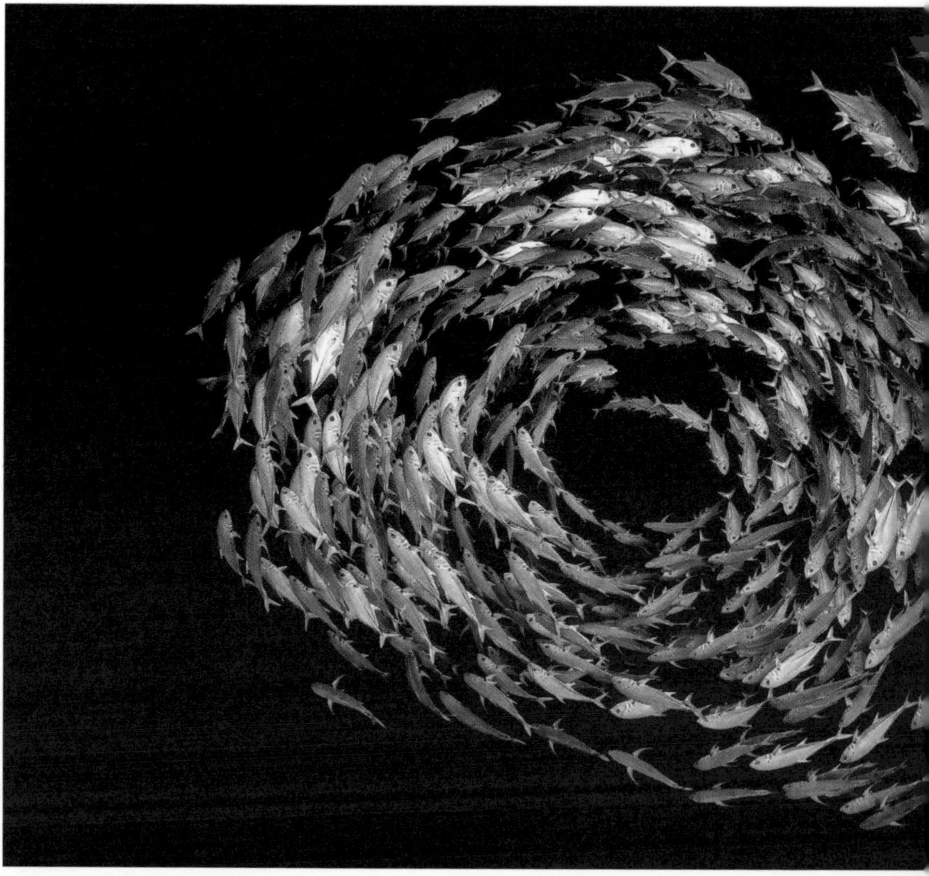

RECIPE FOR SUCCESS

Your final assignment is to enter your photos into a photo contest. Contests often have generous prizes and will help you improve as a photographer. They are a great way to chart your progress and are much more objective than social media "likes." Hopefully, one day, you will be named Underwater Photographer of the Year!

If you want to attract the judges' attention, you need images that jump out. View your contenders on a Lightroom grid—the ones that catch your eye will also appeal to the judges. However, in big contests, your shot needs staying power to last through the rounds, so the thumbnail needs to get even better when viewed at size, rather than just feeling like the same shot seen larger. The other way to stand out is to be different. Don't enter what is fashionable. Instead, go your own way and enter shots that only you have, whether this is with subjects, locations, or techniques.

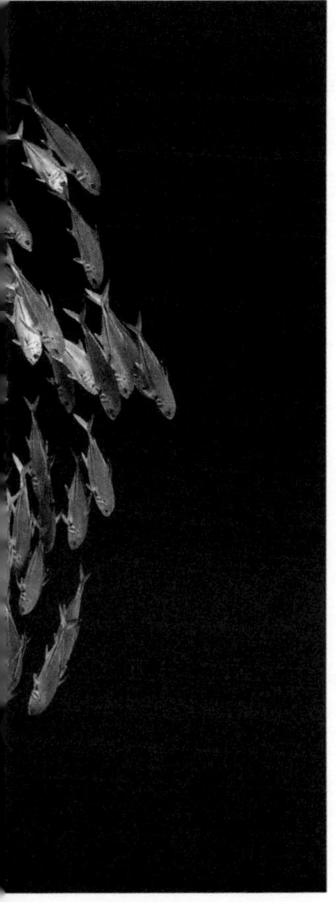

Never give the judges a reason to knock your images out. Read the rules carefully and follow them, taking care to process your images to the best of your ability, without oversaturating or oversharpening. Always respect the wildlife and wild places in the shots because no contest wants to award unethical shots. Make sure your images don't have minor flaws—there are many photos where the focus is sharp enough for social media, but not contest inspection. Don't copy previous winners, even if you took the shot first. Don't spam the judges with lots of similar shots, as you will reduce the chances of any of the pictures doing well. And finally, give yourself plenty of time to enter. One of the most common things you hear when contests announce their results is, "I've got a shot like that." That's a win that slipped through your fingers!

◄ *Viewed small, this image catches the eye. Seen bigger, it is packed with interest, and is ideal for negotiating the rounds of a contest. It was highly commended in the Wildlife Photographer of the Year competition and displayed at 10 Downing Street, our Prime Minister's residence.*

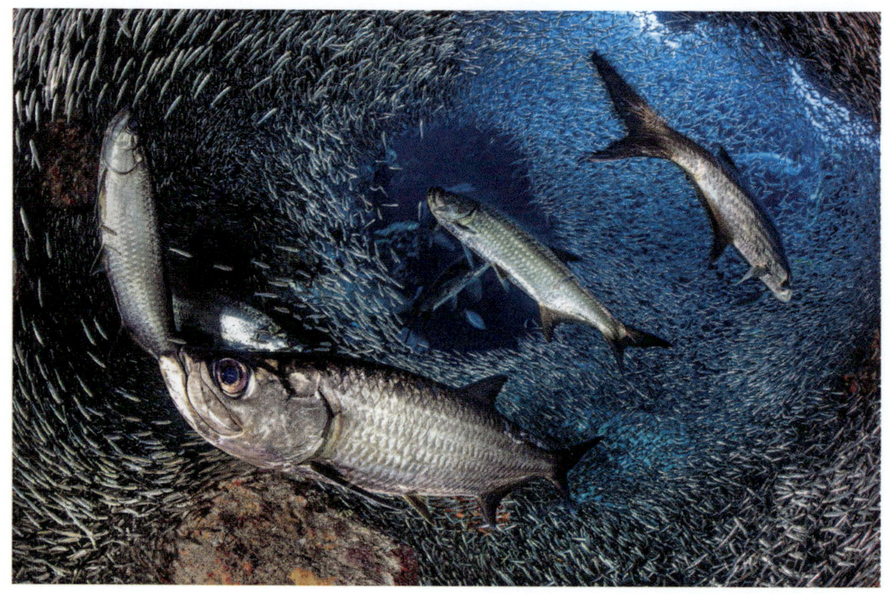

PRO TIPS

- Many photographers worry that sharing shots on social media will harm their chances. I don't believe this because you always see shots win multiple awards and previous success rarely harms their chances. That said, it is always great to win with an image that nobody knows you have taken.

- Photographers are notoriously poor at picking their own pictures, as it is hard to disassociate the effort and desire for a shot from its appeal to competition judges who know nothing of the backstory. If a contest lets you enter 10 shots, try choosing five yourself, then invite a photography friend to choose your other five, and see whose selection of your pictures does best.

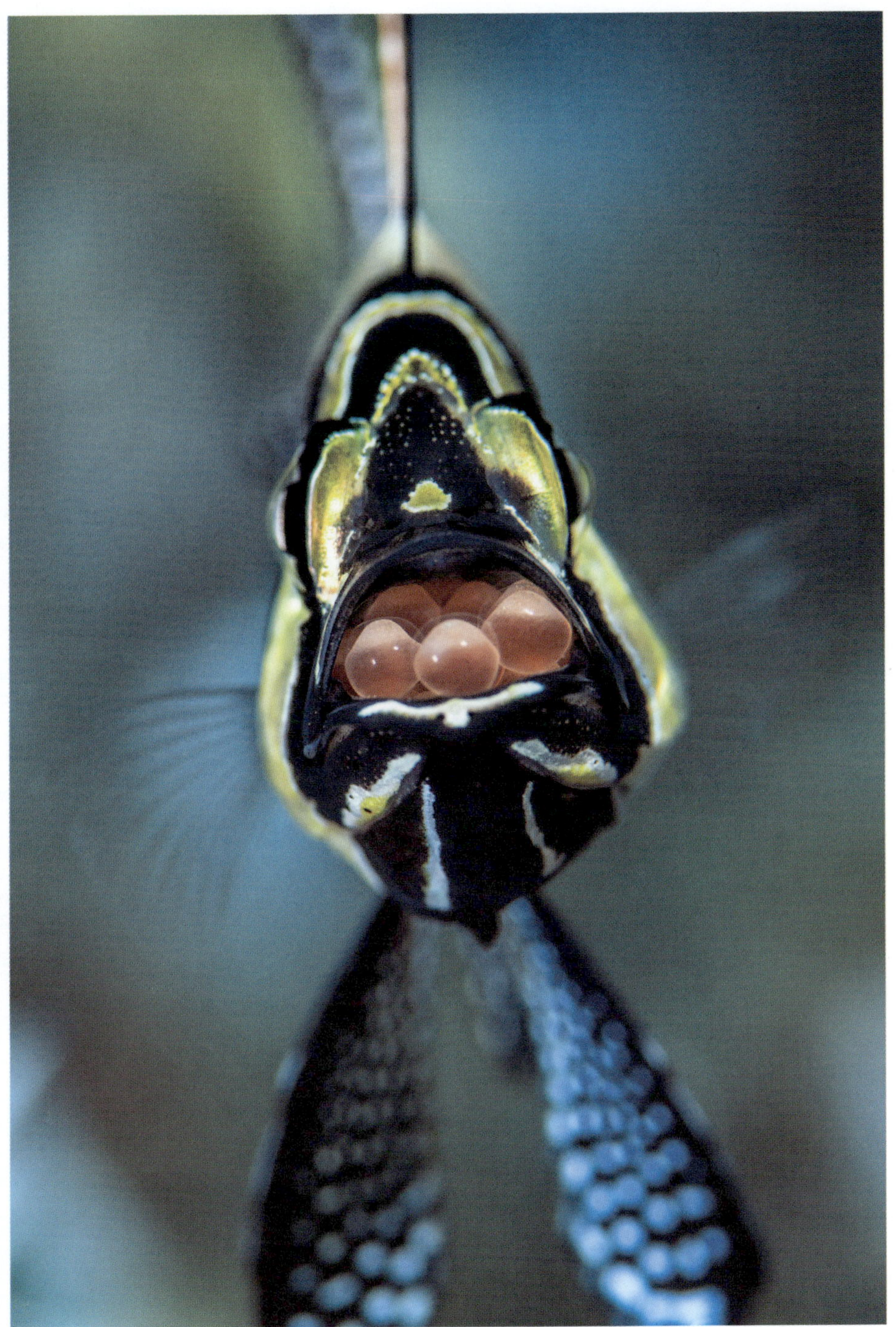

INDEX

A
anemone 74
anemonefish 39, 74
anthias 21, 40, 88, 103
aperture 32, 34, 38, 40–41, 46, 55, 62, 64,
    66, 68, 74, 95, 100, 103, 105
approaching animals 11, 13, 39
aspect ratio 107, 119
autofocus 14, 52–53, 54, 56, 62, 71, 88

B
back-button focus 62, 64, 90
backgrounds 13, 21, 30, 36, 39, 40–41,
    51, 66, 68, 73, 76–77, 81, 82–83, 90–91,
    92–93, 96
backlight 79, 90–91
beam restrictor 18, 90
behavior, photographing 54–55, 114–115,
    124
big animals 8, 39, 44, 56
bioluminescence 92
black-and-white 26–27
blackwater photography 56–57
blennies 28, 88
blur 94–95, 100–101
bokeh 41, 96, 103
bryozoans 34
buddy, dive 14, 24, 47, 82–83, 85, 86–87,
    112–113, 121

C
camera angle 9, 12–13, 26–27, 28, 34, 51,
    54, 74, 76, 80–81, 108
camera housing 11, 14, 18, 24, 28, 44, 56,
    71, 88, 113
clouds 8, 25, 30, 51, 105
color 20–23, 30–31, 34, 36–37, 48, 66,
    80–81, 86, 92–93, 105, 119, 121
coral reefs 8, 15, 20–21, 24, 36, 47, 54–55,
    59, 62, 76, 93, 96, 101, 105, 115
corals 24, 34, 36, 49, 76, 92–93

D
depth of field 32–33, 34, 38, 47, 55, 68, 71,
    74, 102, 116
dolphins 24
dome ports 11, 16, 39, 44, 92, 105
double exposure 96–99

E
emotion 20, 88
ethics 72, 123
exposure 8, 24, 30–31, 32, 39, 50–51, 66,
    78, 92, 94–95, 100–101, 108, 112
extension tubes 41
eye contact 13, 28, 88–89

F
fear of missing out 8
filters 40, 80–81, 92, 102
flashlight 112–113
fluorescence 92–93
focus peaking 41
focusing light 54, 56
45° viewfinder 12, 28, 46
framing 25, 30
freedivers 8
frogfish 28, 38–39, 85, 97
front fill 91
front-curtain flash sync 66, 94, 101

G
ghost pipefish 116
glassfish 40, 62
gobies 66, 70, 88
guides, dive 64, 72–73

H
high-speed sync (HSS) 102–103
horizontal orientation 28, 48

I
in-body image stabilization (IBIS) 62
intentional camera movement (ICM) 66
ISO 32, 38–39, 62, 66, 92, 95, 101, 103,
    105, 113

J
jellyfish 10–11, 56

K
kelp 8–9

L
lens
    fisheye 16, 39, 44–45, 50, 76, 81, 92,
        106

mechanical 40–43
wet 106, 110
zoom 36, 48–49
light
ambient 8–9, 10, 27, 32, 36, 38–39,
44–45, 49, 54, 62, 76, 78, 80–81, 95
direction of 8–9, 10, 18–19, 73, 80, 113
lumpsuckers 90

M
macro photography 13, 18, 24, 32, 34,
38–39, 41, 53, 54, 56, 68, 70–71, 73,
74–75, 91, 92, 96, 102–103, 112–113,
116–117
mandarinfish 54–55
mantas 24
model 82–85, 86–87
moray eels 39
muck diving 18, 28, 64
multiple exposure 96–99

N
negative space 66, 68
neutral density (ND) filters 40, 102
night diving 56–57, 66, 113
nudibranchs 28, 65, 117, 121

O
octopus 39, 56
off-camera flash 78–79, 91
overexposure 30

P
panoramas 106–109
patterns 34–35
pelagic action 8, 56
photogrammetry 110–111
plankton 56
post-processing 20, 27, 80–81, 92

R
rash vest 86
reflections 10, 48–49
rock formations 62

S
Saint-Exupéry, Antoine de 68
schools of fish 24, 95, 98

scorpionfish 39
sea cucumbers 34, 74
sea fans 74, 76
sea lions 24, 95, 115
sea slugs 69, 70,
sea squirts 34
seahorses 28, 74
seaweeds 8–9, 47, 49
shadows 26
sharks 15, 95
shrimps 74
shutter speed 8, 30, 32, 36, 39, 62, 64, 66,
95, 101, 103, 105, 113
silhouettes 24–25, 36, 82, 85, 96, 98
silverside 124
small animals 12
Snell's window 10, 25, 48, 50–51
snoot 64–65, 66–67, 68, 73, 97
split-level photography 46–47, 49,
104–105
sponges 34, 36
starfish 34, 115
strobes 11, 16, 18–19, 28, 32, 36, 38–39,
44, 64, 78–79
sun 24–25, 30, 36, 39, 44–45, 47, 51, 54,
58–61, 80, 99, 104–105
supermacro photography 70–71
swimming technique 11
symbiosis 74, 115

T
tarpon 124
turtles 24, 51, 116

V
vertical orientation 28–29

W
white balance 80, 108
wideangle macro (WAM) 38–39
wideangle photography 13, 14, 24, 30–31,
36, 38–39, 51, 56, 63, 76, 82, 85, 86, 92,
95, 96, 102–103, 116–117
wrecks 8, 24, 26–27, 44, 78, 80–81,
110–111, 115, 121

Z
zoom blur 100–101, 116

First published 2024 by
Ammonite Press
an imprint of Guild of Master Craftsman Publications Ltd
Castle Place, 166 High Street, Lewes, East Sussex, BN7 1XU,
United Kingdom

Text and images © Alex Mustard, 2024
Copyright in the Work © GMC Publications Ltd, 2024

ISBN 978-1-78145-489-3

A catalog record for this book is available from the British Library.

Publisher: Jonathan Bailey
Production Director: Jim Bulley
Design Manager: Robin Shields
Senior Project Editor: Tom Kitch
Editor: Ben Hawkins

Color reproduction by GMC Reprographics
Printed and bound in China

DEDICATION
This book is dedicated to the memory of my good friend, the great Martin Edge,
who would have loved taking on all these challenges.

How was the book?
Please post your
feedback and photos:
#52AssignmentsUnderwater

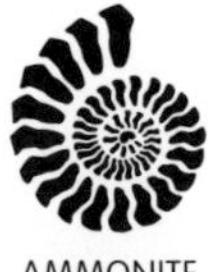

ammonitepress.com

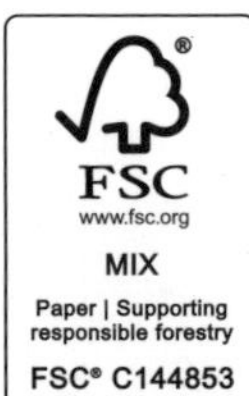